YALE

SHAKESPEARE

SUPPLEMENTS

YALE SHAKESPEARE SUPPLEMENTS

A. M. Nagler. Shakespeare's Stage
Helge Kökeritz. Shakespeare's Names:

> *A Pronouncing Dictionary*

BY THE SAME AUTHOR:
YALE UNIVERSITY PRESS
Shakespeare's Pronunciation
Mr. William Shakespeares Comedies,
> *Histories, & Tragedies.* A facsimile edition.

OTHER PUBLISHERS
The Phonology of the Suffolk Dialect,
> *Descriptive and Historical*

The Place-Names of the Isle of Wight
Mather Flint on Early Eighteenth-
> *Century English Pronunciation*

A Guide to Chaucer's Pronunciation

LP PHONOGRAPH RECORDS
Shakespeare's Pronunciation
Beowulf and Chaucer (with John C. Pope)

SHAKESPEARE'S NAMES·

A PRONOUNCING

DICTIONARY

by HELGE KÖKERITZ

YALE UNIVERSITY PRESS

NEW HAVEN AND LONDON

Originally set in Monotype Series 7 and 72,
and printed in Sweden in 1959 by
Almqvist & Wiksells Boktryckeri AB, Uppsala

Fifth printing, 1977.
Printed in the United States of America
by Alpine Press,
South Braintree, Massachusetts

ISBN: 0–300–00637–3.

Published in Great Britain, Europe, Africa, and
Asia (except Japan) by Yale University Press, Ltd.,
London. Distributed in Latin America by Kaiman
& Polon, Inc., New York City; in Australia and
New Zealand by Book & Film Services, Artarmon,
N.S.W., Australia; and in Japan by Harper & Row,
Publishers, Tokyo Office.

PREFACE

Practical purposes have motivated the compilation of this little manual, which in a sense supplements my *Shakespeare's Pronunciation*, New Haven, Yale University Press, 1953. The latter volume examined a few dozen Shakespearean names of phonological interest but omitted the rest as not falling properly within its field of inquiry. Here therefore are all the proper names in Shakespeare's works, alphabetically arranged and provided with phonetic transcriptions showing at a glance the pronunciation of each, with particular attention to metrical variants. The Elizabethan pronunciation of the names, if different from present-day usage, has also been indicated throughout. A book of this kind should, I trust, prove as helpful for directors and actors as for teachers and students of Shakespeare.

Professor Harold Orton of Leeds has gone through the manuscript and made valuable suggestions, which have been gratefully incorporated. With Dr. Olof von Feilitzen of the Royal Library, Stockholm, I have had the privilege of discussing the etymologies of some obscure names, and Mr. Stanley Ellis, M.A., of Leeds has been kind enough to find out for me the local pronunciation of a Gloucestershire name. I thank them all for helping me to make this book a reliable source of information.

H. K.

CONTENTS

ABBREVIATIONS

Works

AC	Antony and Cleopatra
AW	All's Well That Ends Well
AYL	As You Like It
C	Coriolanus
CE	The Comedy of Errors
Cy	Cymbeline
H	Hamlet
1H4	First Part of Henry IV
2H4	Second Part of Henry IV
H5	Henry V
1H6	First Part of Henry VI
2H6	Second Part of Henry VI
3H6	Third Part of Henry VI
H8	Henry VIII
J	King John

JC	Julius Caesar
L	King Lear
LLL	Love's Labour's Lost
M	Macbeth
MA	Much Ado about Nothing
MM	Measure for Measure
MND	A Midsummer Night's Dream
MV	The Merchant of Venice
MWW	The Merry Wives of Windsor
O	Othello
P	Pericles
R2	Richard II
R3	Richard III
RJ	Romeo and Juliet
RL	The Rape of Lucrece
T	The Tempest
TA	Titus Andronicus
TC	Troilus and Cressida
TGV	The Two Gentlemen of Verona
TmA	Timon of Athens
TN	Twelfth Night
TNK	The Two Noble Kinsmen
TS	The Taming of the Shrew
VA	Venus and Adonis
WT	The Winter's Tale

Other

A	American English
Br.E.	British English
F	First Folio
Fr	(modern) French

G	(modern) German
It	(modern) Italian
L	Latin
OED	*The Oxford English Dictionary*
OFr	Old French
ON	Old Norse
PN Np	*The Place-Names of Northamptonshire*[1]
PN Wa	*The Place-Names of Warwickshire*[1]
PN YE	*The Place-Names of the East Riding of Yorkshire*[1]
pr.	prologue *or* induction
Q	First Quarto
Q2	Second Quarto
S	Shakespeare(an)
Sc	Scottish
SD	stage direction
Sh.Pr.	Kökeritz, *Shakespeare's Pronunciation*, New Haven, 1953
Sp	(modern) Spanish

$(2 \times)$, $(3 \times)$, etc. after a name indicate the number of times it occurs.

A colon between italicized words shows rhyme: *be:me.*

[1] Published by the English Place-Name Society, Cambridge: Vol. 10, 1933; 13, 1936; 14, 1937.

PHONETIC SYMBOLS

Vowels and Diphthongs

[a]   as in Fr *patte* [pat], G *Mann* [man], or It *pasta* ['pasta][1]
[a:] as in Fr *art* [a:r]
[ɑ:] as in *father* ['fɑ:ðər]
[ai] as *i* in *like* [laik]
[au] as *ou* in *house* [haus]
[æ]   as *a* in *bad* [bæd]
[e]   as *e* in *bed* [bed]
[e:] as *ä* in G *Träne* ['tre:nə]
[ei] as *a* in *take* [teik]

---

[1] Since these three short *a*'s are very similar, if not identical
(see e.g. Otto Jespersen, *Lehrbuch der Phonetik*, 2d ed. Leipzig
and Berlin, 1912, §§ 9.93 f., and R. M. S. Heffner, *General
Phonetics*, Madison, Wisc., 1952, pp. 102–3), they are transcribed
with the same phonetic symbol.

[ẹ] as *é* in Fr *été* [ẹtẹ]

[ə] as *a* in *about* [əˈbaut], *o* in *gallop* [ˈgæləp]

[əː] as *ir* in Br.E. *bird* [bəːd]

[əi] an [ə] sound followed by nonsyllabic [i]

[əu] an [ə] sound followed by nonsyllabic [u]

[ɛ] as in Fr *dette* [dɛt]

[ɛː] as in Fr *même* [mɛːm]

[ɛə] as *ere* in Br.E. *there* [ðɛə]

[i] as *i* and *y* in *city* [ˈsiti] (see p. 14)

[iː] as *ee* in *see* [siː]

[iə] as *ere* in Br.E. *here* [hiə]

[o] as *o* in Br.E. *obey* [oˈbei]

[oː] as *o* in G *Sohn* [zoːn], Fr *chose* [ʃoːz]

[ou] as *o* in *go* [gou], *ow* in *know* [nou]

[ɔ] as *o* in both Br.E. and A *hot* [hɔt] (see p. 15)

[ɔː] as *aw* in *law* [lɔː]²

[ø] as *eu* in Fr *peu* [pø]

[œː] as *eu* in Fr *peur* [pœːr]

[u] as *oo* in *good* [gud]

[uː] as *oo* in *moon* [muːn]

[ʌ] as *u* in *cut* [kʌt]

[y] as *u* in Fr *duc* [dyk]

Consonants

[b] as in *bad* [bæd]

[d] as in *day* [dei]

[dʒ] as *dg* in *bridge* [bridʒ]

[f] as in *fee* [fiː]

---

² [ɔ] and [ɔː] will be used also for the Fr vowels in *comme* [kɔm] and *fort* [fɔːr] respectively.

[g]   as in *gay* [gei]
[h]   as in *how* [hau]
[hw] as *wh* in A *when* [hwen]
[j]   as *y* in *yes* [jes]
[k]   as in *kin* [kin]
[l]   as in *let* [let]
[m]   as in *my* [mai]
[n]   as in *name* [neim]
[ŋ]   as *ng* in *sing* [siŋ]
[ɲ]   as *gn* in Fr *vigne* [viɲ]
[p]   as in *paw* [pɔ:]
[r]   as in *ripe* [raip], *very* [ˈveri][3]
[*r*] as in *far* [fɑːr] (see p. 13)
[s]   as in *seal* [si:l]
[ʃ]   as *sh* in *ship* [ʃip]
[t]   as in *tea* [ti:]
[tʃ] as *ch* in *church* [tʃəːrtʃ]
[θ]   as *th* in *thin* [θin]
[ð]   as *th* in *then* [ðen]
[v]   as in *vat* [væt]
[w]   as in *wine* [wain]
[x]   as *ch* in G *ach* [ax], Sc *loch* [lɔx]
[z]   as in *zeal* [zi:l]
[ʒ]   as *s* in *pleasure* [ˈpleʒər]

General Symbols

Optional sounds (e.g. as described on p. 12) are indicated
    by italicized symbols.
[ˈ]   before a syllable indicates strong (primary) stress.

   [3] I.e. as in either British or American English; [r] is also used
for the totally different **Fr**, **It**, and **Sp** *r* sounds.

[ˌ]   before a syllable indicates secondary stress.

[:]   after a vowel indicates full length.[4]

[(:)] after a vowel indicates vacillation in length (short·
       long).[4]

[·]   after a vowel indicates half length.

[ˌ]   below *l, m, n* means that the consonant is syllabic.

[~]   above a vowel indicates nasalization, as in Fr *on* [ɔ̃],
       un [œ̃], *vin* [vɛ̃].

(?) after a transcription indicates a hypothetical form.

For further discussion of the use of italics and parentheses
       see p. 12 below.

---

4 For exceptions see p. 15.

INTRODUCTION

The object of this volume is to make available to the general reader, and above all to teachers, students, and actors, a reliable guide to the pronunciation of all the proper names in Shakespeare's works, including his poems as well as *Pericles* and *The Two Noble Kinsmen*. It will show first of all how these names are commonly pronounced today in both England and America and how they should be pronounced at certain times in order to comply with the rhythm of Shakespeare's verse, for his usage was not always identical with ours. Moreover, it will indicate the approximate pronunciation of the names in Shakespeare's own day, as an aid to the student of his language and prosody. Since the aim is purely practical, the names have been arranged alphabetically, and their prosodically and historically significant variants —which are all recorded here—have as a rule been provided with precise references to act, scene, and line of the

1

respective play or plays, as well as with other pertinent information when so required. Furthermore, several names, mainly those which present problems of identification or have some special interest, have been dealt with at some length in this introduction.

This is consequently a pronouncing dictionary recording some 1800 names in Shakespeare's works. In the main it follows the general arrangement of such well-known handbooks as Daniel Jones, *An English Pronouncing Dictionary*, and Kenyon-Knott, *A Pronouncing Dictionary of American English*, which actually list a great many Shakespearean names. But it differs from these by its comprehensiveness, by its full treatment of metrical and phonological variants, and by including in one volume three types of pronunciation: British, American, and Elizabethan. On the whole, the pronunciations shown here agree with those of Jones, Kenyon-Knott, and others. When, however, I have been driven by etymological or phonological reasons to deviate from what may, rightly or wrongly, be called the received pronunciation, the fact has been duly noted at the entry in question. Yet many names, mostly of foreign extraction or dubious provenance, are unrecorded in the standard pronouncing dictionaries, so that in such cases the author of a guide like this is forced to suggest phonologically and metrically justifiable pronunciations in the hope that they will not violate any long-standing oral tradition.

Every name has its own history, it has become an integral part of our whole cultural heritage, and its origin and structure must therefore be closely examined before we can commend or reject a particular pronunciation. The current stage pronunciations of names like *Jaques* and *Verges*, namely [ˈdʒeikwi(ː)z] and [ˈvəːrdʒi(ː)z], clearly show a break with Shakespeare's usage: the contemporary form of *Jaques* would contain no [w], while *-es* in both names would be sounded [is]; and the Elizabethan actor and his audience knew that *Verges* was the common colloquial form of *verjuice*, often spelled *verges*, *vergis*, *vergesse* in the 16th and 17th centuries. The present-day forms are comparatively recent spelling pronunciations, probably dating back to the 18th century. Thus it would be unwise to pay much heed to the pronunciations used or recommended by modern actors and actresses, for their ideas of "correctness" or "effectiveness" are usually purely impressionistic and without supporting linguistic evidence. An actor or reciter—or for that matter any reader of Shakespeare— is of course fully justified in regarding a certain pronunciation as more beautiful or musical than another. But if the "beautiful" or "musical" variant violates the sound system of English or of the language from which the name ultimately comes, if it ignores the exigencies of Shakespeare's verse, or if it disregards significant phonological facts, then it is nothing but a distortion and should not be tolerated.[1] To accept the principle of the beautiful

---

[1] Many fanciful pronunciations of this kind by prominent actors and actresses of the past and present figure in Theodora Irvine, *A Pronouncing Dictionary of Shakespearean Proper Names* (New York, 1919, 2d ed. 1947), which fondly records them as if they were nuggets of gold. In a recent college production of *King Lear*, the actors had been coached by their student director to say [ˈreigən] for *Regan* because the name appears as *Ragan* in *The True Chronicle History of King Leir* (1605), one of Shakespeare's sources. In Holinshed, however, and in Spenser's *Faerie Queene*, which Shakespeare also used, the name is *Regan*; and still earlier,

or musical impression as a guide to the pronunciation of a name would be as unrealistic as, say, to recommend the pronunciation [ˈjuːɡlai] for *ugly* because it might sound less ugly than [ˈʌgli]. Indeed, no phonetically beautiful or ugly words or names exist in any language; it is the nonphonetic associations they evoke which may be pleasant or unpleasant, gay or sad, refined or vulgar—but never the sound sequences themselves. When today, for instance, we hear *Henry* pronounced [ˈhenəri] instead of [ˈhenri], we immediately identify the former variant with a certain social group; yet phonetically speaking, the sole difference between the two is the medial [ə] in [ˈhenəri], which is certainly not an uneducated or vulgar sound in itself. The irony of it is that we simply must use [ˈhenəri] at times (see p. 58) in order to do justice to Shakespeare's verse; to him, obviously, the trisyllabic form carried no stigma of vulgarity. Or, to take another example, who can decide whether [taiˈteiniə] or [tiˈtɑːniə] is the more euphonious pronunciation of *Titania*? Since the two variants are equally acceptable, the choice between them is entirely free, but it is not certain that the user's preference will coincide with the hearer's. Thus when a free choice exists between fully acceptable variants the whole problem becomes one of personal taste, and no valid objection can be raised to the use of a particular variant. But any deliberate distortion of a name or a word on the assumption that artificiality is synonymous

in *Laȝamon's Brut* (13th century) we find both *Ragau* and *Regau*. Even if it could be proved that Shakespeare said [ˈreːɡən] for *Regan*, there would be as little reason for retaining such a pronunciation today as there would be for us to adopt his [ˈseːzər] instead of present-day [ˈsiːzər] (*Caesar*).

with euphony or effectiveness should be branded as an outrage upon the English language.[2]

Here it may be appropriate to discuss briefly the question to what extent the pronunciation of a foreign name should be anglicized. English has for centuries treated frequently used foreign names as if they were native ones; or, to put it differently, English sounds— and often English stress usages—have been substituted for unfamiliar foreign ones. Such sound substitution is the reason why *Paris* is [ˈpæris] today and not [pari], *Marseilles* [mɑːrˈseilz] and not [marsɛːj], *Quixote* [ˈkwiksət] rather than [kiˈhouti] (although the latter is apparently preferred in America) or [kiˈxote], *Berlin* [bəːrˈlin] and not [bɛrˈliːn], and so on. In some cases, earlier forms of the foreign name still prevail in English, as in *Leghorn* [ˈlegˈhɔːrn] for *Livorno* or old-fashioned [ˈkælis] for *Calais* (cf. Shakespeare's *Callis* and the term *callis-sand*). Similarly, until fairly recently, Latin was normally pronounced in an English fashion, a practice that accounts for such established pronunciations as *Caesar*, *Darius*, *Flavius*, *Ligarius*, *Titus*. Indeed, this is a precedent well worth following for Shakespearean names whenever practicable, except possibly in the case of names of rare or single occurrence, like *Bourgogne* (alongside of anglicized *Burgundy*), *Foix*, *Guysors*, and *Lestrale*; for most of these, however, I have suggested anglicized pronuncia-

---

[2] It is indeed irritating to hear e.g. *Conrade*, an early spelling of *Conrad*, in *Much Ado about Nothing* twisted into a pseudo-Spanish [kɔnˈrɑːdə], and *Messina* in the same play (5.4.128) erroneously accented ◡́ ◡ ◡̀ because neither the director nor the actor seemed to be aware that *armed* in that line ("And brought with armed men back to Messina") is disyllabic [ˈɑːrmid].

tions. The fact that very often French and Italian names are only partially anglicized has resulted in an incongruous treatment of certain Italian final syllables as compared with their direct Latin counterparts, e.g. *-anio* (L *-anius*), *-ano* (L *-anus*), *-ato* (L *-atus*), and *-ario* (L *-arius*). Thus we are accustomed to pronouncing *Bassanio* [bə'sɑ:niou] but *Ascanius* [æs'keiniəs], *Gratiano* [ˌgreiʃi'ɑ:nou] but *Coriolanus* [ˌkɔriə'leinəs], *Leonato* [li(:)ə'nɑ:tou] but *Leonatus* [li(:)ə'neitəs], and *Bellario* [bə'lɑ:riou] but *Belarius* [bə'lɛəriəs]. In other words, we use a pseudo-Italian [ɑ:][3]—in fact, almost the only "Italian" element in any of these names—where consistency would seem to favor the same pronunciation as in the corresponding Latin suffixes. Yet the practice appears to be so firmly entrenched that it would perhaps be unrealistic to suggest a fully anglicized pronunciation of these and other Italian names.

The pronunciation of several names cannot be determined with any degree of certainty. In such cases anglicization would, it seems, be the safest procedure. Take for instance *Amurath* 2H4 5.2.48: the only thing we know for certain about it is its stress on the first syllable, but we cannot now tell whether in Shakespeare's time the two *a*'s were sounded [æ] or [a], though the former appears the more likely alternative and is definitely preferable to the current [ɑ]. That [æ] should be used in *Valdes* P 4.1.97 is obvious also, but there is as little reason for pronouncing its final *-es* [i:z] (on the analogy of *Hercules*) as there is for doing so in *Jaques* and *Verges*. *Valdes* is surely not a Greek name: it has a Spanish flavor

---

[3] The standard Italian vowel is, of course, [a:].

and may actually refer to some contemporary pirate. The final syllable should therefore be [is] or perhaps [əs]—cf. the two alternate forms *Veroles* and *Verollus*. Etymologically, the *e* in *Sweno* M 1.2.59, which is a Scandinavian name (ON *Sveinn,* modern Swedish *Sven*), should be [e], but [i:] seems an acceptable English substitute for it. The same vowel may consequently be used in *Nedar* MND 1.1.107, 4.1.133 as well as in *Chetas* TC pr.16, whose initial *ch*, on the other hand, should be [k] as in other anglicized Greek names. Favoring [ɔ] in *Brocas* R2 5.6.14 is the F spelling *Broccas*. Either [i] or [ai] may be used in *Sinel* M 1.3.71 (a mistranscription of original *Finele*), though its Scottish origin favors [i]. *Sowter* TN 2.5.135, the name of a dog, is usually given with northern [u:] (cf. *souter*, OED), but since the word was common all over England in Old and Middle English times, we may well assume that it was indigenous to southern England in Shakespeare's time and was therefore pronounced [ˈsəutər], giving [ˈsautər] today.

Undue regard for the spelling, on the other hand, has resulted in [ˈkeipl] for *Capel* RJ 5.1.18, 5.3.127, which, since it is an apocopated metrical variant of *Capulet*, should be pronounced [ˈkæpl] and not like the etymologically unrelated surname *Capel(l)*.

Three names are of particular interest because of the problems of identification involved. The first is *Chus* MV 3.2.285, the name of a friend of Shylock's. *Chus* is clearly a variant of *Cush*, son of Ham (Genesis 10.6–8 and 1 Chronicles 1.8–10),[4] which actually appears as Χούς in the Greek text; since Greek χ is regularly transliterated

---

[4] In Genesis 10.2 and 1 Chronicles 1.5 we find *Tubal*, the name of another friend of Shylock's, mentioned together with *Chus*.

ch in English, it is not surprising to find *Chus* for *Cush* in *The Bishop's Bible* of 1572, with which Shakespeare was no doubt familiar; *The Geneva Bible* of 1560, however, has *Cush*. For the *ch* of *Chus* [k] should be used, with *u* as [ʌ] or [u] unless the current form *Cush* [kʌʃ] is preferred.

Swithold (spelled *Swithald* Q) in the incantation recited by Edgar in L 3.4.125 is usually taken to be a misprint for *S. Withold*, i.e. St. Withold. Since no St. Withold is recorded elsewhere—though we have evidence of a Continental-Germanic name *Witold*—commentators have conjectured that *Swithold* is a corruption of *St. Vitalis*; but this is not very likely phonologically. Dr. Olof von Feilitzen has, however, called my attention to the Old English name *Swiðweald* in the *Liber Vitae* (ca. 800), whose first element is identical with that of *Swithin*: in Middle English and early Modern English, *Swiðweald* would regularly appear as *Swithold* or *Swithald*. Such a name may well have survived in an ancient charm of the kind used by Edgar. Whatever the origin of *Swithold* or *St. Withold*, the quality of its medial *th* is doubtful: it may be [ð], [θ], or even [t], should the name be connected with Germanic *Witold* or prove to be, after all, an anglicized form of *Vitalis*.

Woncot 2H4 5.1.42 has been identified with both Woodmancote, a suburb of Dursley in Gloucestershire, and Wilnecote in Warwickshire, which appears as *Wincot* TS pr.2.23. Tending to favor Woodmancote are the facts that the 2H4 passage mentions William Visor and Clement Perkes and that families named Visor and Perkes actually lived in that neighborhood in the 16th century.[5] Richard

---

[5] For details see the *Variorum Ed.*, p. 392.

W. Huntley's statement[6] that in the 1860's Woodmancote was still pronounced "Womcot" by common people points to a pronunciation [ˈwɔmkət] or, more likely, [ˈumkət], although no such form is recognized there today; according to Mr. Stanley Ellis of the University of Leeds, the current local pronunciations are [ˈudmən‿kwət] and [ˈudmən‿kɔt]. Irrespective of whether *Woncot* is identical with Woodmancote or Wilnecote,[7] the Shakespearean form suggests a pronunciation [ˈ(w)uŋkət] or [ˈwɔŋkət].

EXPLANATIONS

To the proper names included here, I have added an occasional proper noun or adjective like *Goth, Nemean.* Each is recorded only once, regardless of whether it is borne by one or (as in the case of *Henry*) a dozen individuals, since obviously its frequency in Shakespeare does not affect its pronunciation—though its prosodic use may at times do so (see e.g. *Henry,* which is sometimes trisyllabic). No references have been given to the occurrence of a particular name in the text except when, say, its number of syllables in a given line or the use of a particular variant needs to be indicated: see such entries as *Abergavenny, Abraham, Ajax, Jaques.* The precise location of a name can be easily ascertained from Bartlett's

[6] *A Glossary of the Cotswold (Gloucestershire) Dialect* (London, 1868), p. 22.

[7] In my *Shakespeare's Pronunciation* (New Haven, 1953), p. 215, I identify *Woncot* with *Wilnecote* and explain its *o* as a case of rounding of *i* after *w.*

Concordance, with the exception of names appearing in stage directions or in *The Two Noble Kinsmen*, which are not recorded there.

As a rule, names are spelled in the way they appear in modern Shakespeare editions; where some other form has been preferred, the traditional one has usually also been added with a reference to the former (see e.g. *Salanio*). Variations in the F and Q spellings have been noted only when they seem to be phonologically significant, as in the case of *Abergavenny, Cophetua, Eleanor*. Obviously corrupt F spellings like *Antenonidus* for *Antenorides* have been ignored. Identifications of unusual name forms have been provided within parentheses after the main entry, as in *Ciceter, Guynes, Wallon*.

The line numbering is that of *The Complete Works of Shakespeare*, edited by George Lyman Kittredge,[8] which agrees closely with that of the Globe edition.

The phonetic alphabet used is the International Phonetic Association (IPA) alphabet in its "broad" form as successfully employed by Daniel Jones in *An English Pronouncing Dictionary*. Its inherent simplicity and small number of new and strange symbols make it very easy for anyone to grasp quickly, while its largely phonemic character makes it flexible enough to render satisfactorily both British and American pronunciations, as well as any differing Elizabethan ones, without adding extra symbols. A key to the phonetic symbols appears on pp. XIII ff., and the principles followed in distinguishing certain American and Elizabethan variants from the corresponding British forms are explained in full on pp. 13 ff. and 16 ff.

[8] Boston, Ginn and Co., 1936.

Each entry consists of the name in its conventional form followed by one or more phonetic transcriptions. Transcriptions appearing without a preceding *A* or *S* represent pronunciations common to modern British, modern American, and Elizabethan English—either single pronunciations, as in the case of *Adam* and *Elbe*, or variants, as for *Agamemnon* and *Lucilius*. Thus *Cromwell* ['krɔmwəl, 'krʌm-, -wel] implies a choice of four variants, namely ['krɔmwəl, 'krʌmwəl, 'krɔmwel, 'krʌmwel].

An *A* before a transcription indicates a deviating pronunciation heard in present-day American English, while an *S* designates a Shakespearean or Elizabethan variant: see such entries as *Blanch*, *Derby*. If *A* or *S* is followed by +, the transcription indicates a variant in American or Elizabethan English in addition to the ones recorded before it: thus *Alice* ['ælis], *S* + [æls] means that besides ['ælis] Shakespeare used the syncopated variant [æls]; and *Asia* ['eiʃə], *A* + ['eiʒə], *S* ['e:ʃə, 'e:ʃie:] means that the standard British pronunciation ['eiʃə] may be heard in American English as a variant of ['eiʒə] but that ['e:ʃə, 'e:ʃie:] were the regular disyllabic and trisyllabic forms in Elizabethan English (this particular entry specifies moreover the occurrence of the trisyllabic variant).

L, *Fr*, *It*, *Sp* denote respectively variants in Latin and in modern French, Italian, and Spanish: see e.g. *Aeacida*, *Artois*, *Gonzago*, *Adriano de Armado*.

Instead of repeating the full transcription of a name when only part of it differs in a variant, only the syllable or syllables in question will usually be transcribed, preceded and/or followed by a hyphen: see e.g. *Acheron*,

Apemantus, Caithness, Glendower. A hyphen is also used occasionally to mark syllable division, as in *Wiltshire.* Stress variants, without phonetic transcriptions, will be shown in the traditional manner by an acute accent over a dash for primary stress (⌐́) and a grave accent over a dash for secondary stress (⌐̀), as for *Arviragus, Balthazar, Bartholomew.*

By italicizing certain symbols, mainly [*r, t, d, p, i, u*] (see below, p. 13), it has often been possible to combine within one transcription both the British and the American pronunciation of a name, as well as common variants of either; optional [j], [w], [l], prosodic [ə] , and [:] (length) as in *Lucrece, Woncot, Aemilia, Walter, Viola* have instead been enclosed within parentheses. Thus an entry like

Gerard 'dʒeraːrd, 'dʒerəd, dʒəˈraːrd, *S* -raːrd, *Fr* ʒeraːr

should be understood as follows: In both British and American English there are two stress variants, one ⌐́ ⌐, the other ⌐ ⌐́; moreover, in [-*r*d] the [*r*] is usually silent in British English but pronounced in American, a fact shown by the italicized *r*. The Shakespeare form differs from both in the quality of its *a* [aː], while its preconsonantal *r* may perhaps still have been sounded (see p. 17); the hyphen indicates that the first syllable of the name is assumed to have been the same as in the variants used today. The name appears twice in prose, giving no clue to the incidence of stress, and once in verse (AW 2.1.104),[9] where the stress seems to be ⌐ ⌐́. And the modern French form is [ʒeraːr].

[9] Since that line has only nine syllables, it should perhaps be combined with the preceding short line of four syllables into one

Unstressed endings like *-ia, -ian, -ean, -io, -eo, -ium,
-ius, -eus* may be monosyllabic or disyllabic, that is,
either [jə, jən, jou, jəm, jəs] or [iə, iən, iou, iəm, iəs][10]—
or [ʃə, ʒə, tʃə, dʒə], etc. through assibilation. In verse
the scansion of the line will generally suggest the variant
to be used, but in prose either will obviously do. Typical
instances are names like *Aemilia, Charmian, Nemean,
Ariel, Juliet, Bassanio, Ilium, Claudius.* If only [jə] is
given, as in *Bohemia*, only the monosyllabic variant of
such an ending has been recorded from Shakespeare; but
this transcription is of course not intended to preclude
the occurrence of disyllabic forms in [iə] elsewhere.

American Variants

Unless otherwise shown, the transcription of each entry
should be understood to represent the current British
and American pronunciation of that particular name.
This frequent conflation of the two principal phonetic
variants, British and American, has necessitated the use
of the italic symbol [*r*] to render the preconsonantal and
final *r* usually heard in American but not in British
English (as pointed out on p. xv, italicization of a
phonetic symbol indicates an optional sound). Thus

six-foot line with feminine ending: "I my good Lord, Gerard de
Narbon was my father."

[10] There exists also a rising diphthong [iə] (monosyllabic) in
which [ə] is the more sonorous element, but the difference between
this diphthong and [jə], though appreciable to the trained ear
(see e.g. Daniel Jones, *An Outline of English Phonetics*, 8th ed.
Cambridge, 1956, § 466), is so subtle that we need not consider it
here.

13

Arthur [ˈɑːrθər] represents both British [ˈɑːθə] and American [ˈɑ(ː)rθər]. On the other hand, American pronunciation ignores the glide [ə] which appears finally and before pronounced *r* in such British variants as *Lear* [liə], *Ariel* [ˈɛəriəl], *Blackfriars* [ˈblækˈfraiəz], corresponding to American [lir], [ˈɛriəl], [-ˈfrairz]. In these and similar cases, consequently, [ər] in *Lear* [liər], *-friars* [-ˈfraiərz] and [ər] in *Ariel* [ˈɛəriəl] are to be interpreted as American [r].

When an entry contains a transcription preceded by *A*, this transcription alone is the current American variant, and what precedes it should be interpreted as the corresponding British pronunciation. Such entries are, however, very rare; a case in point is *Curan*. More common are transcriptions preceded by *A* +, e.g. *Asia* [ˈeiʃə], *A* + [ˈeiʒə]; as explained on p. 11 above, such an entry means that in addition to [ˈeiʃə] one often hears [ˈeiʒə] in American English. Also, names containing stressed *o(u)r* and *ore*, e.g. *Ford*, *Courtney*, *Shore*, may be heard with both [ɔːr] and, less commonly, [oːr] in American English, but only the former variant has been recorded here; the latter was, however, characteristic of Elizabethan English and will therefore appear as an *S* variant. Similarly, final unstressed *-(e)y* as in *Fury*, *Aubrey* has been consistently rendered [i], even though many Americans use [iː] here.[11]

As in the broad form of the IPA alphabet, a colon — conventional length symbol—is used to indicate a qualitative rather than a quantitative difference between

---

[11] But [i(ː)] is used for the final *-e* of Greek and Latin names like *Hecate*, *Lethe*, whenever there is vacillation in Br.E. between [iː] and [i].

related vowels, as in Br.E. *beat* [bi:t]—*bit* [bit], *food* [fu:d]—*good* [gud], *caught* [kɔ:t]—*cot* [kɔt], and *about* [əˈbaut]—*bird* [bə:d]. In the same way the colon is used for the *ur(r)* in the names *Curan* and *Murray*, which in American English are pronounced with the vowel of *fur*, that is [ə:r], not [ʌr] as in British English. Similarly, the colon will be found within parentheses to render two quantitatively different vowels, namely American [æ] (as in *bad*, *man*) and the corresponding long vowel [æ:] which was probably the sound of Elizabethan *a* before [f, s, θ] in such names as *Bergomask* [-mæ(:)sk], *Falstaff* [-stæ(:)f], and *Castor* [ˈkæ(:)stər].

Note that the symbol [ɔ] covers the qualitatively different vowels of British and American *got*—[gɔt] in British, [gɑt] in American English. Since short [ɔ] does not normally occur in American English, this rendering is unambiguous; an entry like *Bottom* [ˈbɔtəm] is thus to be understood as including the American pronunciation [ˈbɑtəm].

For those familiar with the modified narrow form of the IPA alphabet as employed by Kenyon,[12] the following correspondences between the broad form as applied here to American English and the narrow one in Kenyon may be helpful:

Broad	Narrow	Examples
[i]	[ɪ]	*bit* [bit]—[bɪt]
[i:]	[i]	*beat* [bi:t]—[bit]
[e]	[ɛ]	*get* [get]—[gɛt]
[ei]	[e]	*gate* [geit]—[get]

[12] J. S. Kenyon and T. A. Knott, *A Pronouncing Dictionary of American English*, Springfield, Mass., 1955.

[ɑ:]	[ɑ]	*calm* [kɑ:m]—[kɑm]
[ai]	[aɪ]	*eye* [ai]—[aɪ]
[au]	[aʊ]	*how* [hau]—[haʊ]
[ɔ]	[ɑ]	*got* [gɔt]—[gɑt]
[ɔ:]	[ɔ]	*law* [lɔ:]—[lɔ]
[ou]	[o]	*go* [gou]—[go]
[u]	[ʊ]	*good* [gud]—[gʊd]
[u:]	[u]	*food* [fu:d]—[fud]

With a following *r*:

[iər]	[ɪr]	*ear* [iər]—[ɪr]
[ɛər]	[ɛr]	*air* [ɛər]—[ɛr]
[aiər]	[aɪr]	*hire* [haiər]—[haɪr]
[auər]	[aʊr]	*our* [auər]—[aʊr]
[uər]	[ʊr]	*poor* [puər]—[pʊr]
[ər]	[ɚ]	*acre* ['eikər]—['ekɚ]
[ə:r]	[ɝ]	*err* [ə:r]—[ɝ]

It is hoped that these conflations, which are meant to simplify the transcriptions and make the entries less unwieldy, will not inconvenience American users of the book.

Shakespearean Variants

Transcriptions preceded by *S* are reconstructed pronunciations postulated for Shakespeare's time. The absence of *S* means that the Shakespearean form of the name in question did not, so far as we know, differ from the present-day British and American variants as recorded here: see e.g. *Adam, Helicon, Thisbe*; an italicized *r*, furthermore, may be assumed to have been sounded, as in *Bedford, Berg, Cornwall.* For the meaning of $S+$ see p. 11 above.

These Shakespearean variants have been reconstructed on the basis of the phonological evidence presented in my *Shakespeare's Pronunciation,* which actually incorporates many of them as examples of various sound developments. English pronunciation at the end of the 16th century was on the whole not very different from present-day speech, even though individual words and names may occasionally have differed a good deal from what we are now accustomed to say or hear. Of particular importance is the coalescence of *ea* in *seal, a* in *sale,* and *ai* in *sail* as [e:] (approximately the long sound corresponding to *e* in *get*), all pronounced [se:l] and so at that time homophones, at any rate in the speech of upper-class people. The diphthongs in *like* and *house* had not yet reached the present stages [ai] and [au] but had as their first element a vowel akin to [ə] in *bishop* ['biʃəp] or [ʌ] in *cut.* They are therefore here rendered [əi] and [əu] respectively. On the other hand, modern [ei] in *tale, tail* and [ou] in *no, know* were still monophthongs, namely the long vowels [e:] and [o:]. It is almost impossible to determine whether or not preconsonantal and final *r* as in *farm, far* had ceased to be pronounced about 1600, and for that reason it has been shown here as fully sounded; but see *Shakespeare's Pronunciation,* pp. 314 ff.

In order to limit as much as possible the number of variant transcriptions, the Shakespearean reconstructions of names containing modern [ɑ:r], [ei], and [ou] which aside from these sounds are identical with the present-day forms have usually not been recorded here, since these sounds correspond regularly to Elizabethan [aːr], [eː], and [oː] respectively. Thus it will be easy for the reader to deduce from modern *Barnet* [ˈbɑːrnit], *Bates* [beits], *Echo* [ˈekou] the Shakespearean equivalents [ˈbaːrnit, beːts, ˈekoː].

The F and Q spellings are sometimes helpful in determining the contemporary pronunciation of names. Witness, e.g., *Aburgany* (Abergavenny), *Alce* (Alice), *Callis* (Calais), *Cotsall* (Cotswold), *Daintry* (Daventry), *th'arganian* (Hyrcanian), *Kymmalton* (Kimbolton); note also *Petruchio* and *Borachio*, whose *ch* represents English [tʃ], and *Venti(d)gius* with (*d*)*g* for English [dʒ] (see p. 22 and entries). From rhymes like *Bianca : stay*, *Helena : away*, and *Berowne : moone* we learn that the final *a* of *Bianca*, *Helena*, and other trisyllabic names ending in *a* was [eː] under secondary stress,[13] and that the second syllable of *Berowne* (Q, F; *Biron*, F2–4) was stressed and pronounced with the [uː] of *moon*. In other cases the rhythm of the verse line provides reliable clues to the stress and number of syllables of a name: see such entries as *Andronicus*, *Barabbas*, *Chatillon*, *Lucrece*, and *Anjou*, *Beatrice*, *Eleanor*, *Ravenspurgh*. It is interesting to note that not only *Douglas* and *Henry* could be trisyllabic if the scansion so required, but also *England* and *Ireland* (the latter with [ˈəi-ər-] or [ˈəirə-]). The pun *Jaques–jakes* AYL 3.3.74–5 reveals that *Jaques* was commonly monosyllabic, whereas the scansion of e.g. AYL 2.2.26 proves that it had a metrical variant of two syllables. And in

---

[13] See further my *Shakespeare's Pronunciation*, pp. 174 f. In deference to Shakespeare's verse, the final *a* of such names as *Asia*, *Bianca*, *Helena* when rhyming with words like *away*, *day*, *May* should be pronounced [ei].

Richard Hodges, *The English Primrose* (1644), a spelling book, we discover that e.g. *Jesus* was then pronounced with [e:], not [i:] as today.

Where no phonological evidence of this kind is available, the suggested Shakespearean form has had to be reconstructed from its present-day equivalent with due regard to the origin of the name (if known), to the phonology of Elizabethan English in general, and to the presumed contemporary Latin and French pronunciation. Nevertheless it is impossible to say whether Shakespeare used [a:] or [æ:] for the *a* of names like *Bassanio, Gonzago, Montano, Pisanio,* and *Romano.* For *Quoint* R2 2.1.284 Holinshed has *Coint;* and since *coint,* like *quoint,* is an early variant of *quaint* and the French name is apparently derived from that adjective (OFr *cointe* 'elegant'),[14] the F editors—or Shakespeare himself— seem to have identified Holinshed's *Coint* with English *quoint,* a spelling they preferred. Yet we do not know how the name was then pronounced: [kəint] or [kwəint], [kɔint] or [kwɔint], perhaps even [kwe:nt], the Elizabethan form of modern *quaint.*

Classical and Italian Names

The conflict between the conventional English pronunciation of Latin and Greek and the reconstructed pronunciation now commonly taught in America and continental Europe is of little concern here. Nearly all

---

[14] A. Dauzat, *Les noms de famille de France* (Paris, 1945), p. 189.

classical names in Shakespeare and other authors have for centuries been pronounced in an English fashion, and there is no reason for breaking this long established tradition. Since *Caesar* will doubtless continue to be generally pronounced [ˈsiːzər] and not [ˈkaisar], which would be the historically correct form, then *Naso* (LLL 4.2.127) should certainly be [ˈneizou] and not [ˈnɑːsou] as is sometimes heard. *Caius*, however, appears to have acquired a hybrid Latin-English pronunciation [ˈkaiəs] in Britain, whereas American [ˈkeiəs] accords better with the usual manner of pronouncing Latin *ai*; Shakespeare may therefore have said [ˈkeːəs]. On the other hand, neither [ˈkaiəs] nor [ˈkeiəs] is to be used to render the name of the French physician in MWW, Dr. Caius. Like the name of the founder of Caius College, Cambridge, this *Caius* is merely a fanciful Latin respelling of *Keys*, and it should consequently be pronounced [kiːz] today.[15]

While in Shakespeare *Philippi* is always stressed _ ́ _ as in Latin and never ́ _ _ as in Greek, a few other classical names deviate from Latin or Greek accentuation. Thus *Andronicus* is always stressed _ ́ _ _, *Arviragus* ̀ _ ́ _, *Posthumus* almost consistently _ ́ _ (possibly ́ _ _ Cy 1.1.41, 3.4.251, and 4.2.320, which are all difficult to scan), and *Euphrates* ́ _ ̀ (it occurs only once). *Lepidus* is ́ _ _, except possibly at JC 3.2.269 (perhaps prose) and AC 2.1.14, where a pause after "hearts" will restore the normal accentuation. Only by disregarding the iambic rhythm can we fit the classical accentuation of *Rhodope*

[15] See my article, "Punning Names in Shakespeare," *Modern Language Notes, 65* (1950), 240 f.

(1H6 1.6.22) and *Dercetas* (AC 5.1.5), that is [rɔˈdoupi:] and [ˈdəːrsitəs], into the pentameter line. The scansion shows that *Rhodope* should be metrically stressed ⏑ — ⏑ and probably pronounced [ˈrɔdoupi:],[16] whereas *Dercetas* seems to be stressed — ⏑ —, unless "I am" in the preceding "I am call'd" is to be contracted to *I'm*, with metrically stressed *I*; if we follow the text, however, metrically stressing both "I" and "call'd", the name will have to be pronounced [dərˈsiːtəs]. Nor can the original Greek stress be retained in *Toryne* [tɔˈraini:], which according to North's *Plutarch* (1579) was pronounced like the Greek noun τοϱύνη, hence concealing an ancient pun. The name of the Albanian city of *Toryne* appears twice in AC, namely at 3.7.24 (here spelled *Troine*, an obvious error for *Torine*) and 3.7.56, where the scansion reveals it to be a disyllable stressed on the first syllable; nevertheless it is impossible to say for certain whether we should pronounce it [ˈtɔrin, ˈtɔrain] or [ˈtourin, ˈtourain]. In *Hecate* the final *e* is always silent except once (1H6 3.2.64), and the same vacillation is characteristic of *Andromache* and *Mytilene*. *Pantheon*, occurring twice in Shakespeare, appears to be stressed in two ways (as it is today): at TA 1.1.242 the stress falls on the first syllable, but at TA 1.1.333 on the second. If, however, *the* were inserted before "Pantheon"[17] in the latter line ("Ascend, fair queen, Pantheon"), the accentuation would be the same as in l. 242—a plausible emendation in view of the original Greek form, πάνθειον, though the existence

[16] *Webster's New International Dictionary* (2d ed.) accents the zoological term *Rhodope* in this way.

[17] Cf. J. C. Maxwell, ed., *Titus Andronicus* (Arden Ed. London, 1953), p. 19.

of the Latin variant *Panthēum* (which may have prompted Dr. Johnson's accentuation _ ⸝ _) could have produced the same stress in Shakespeare's time.[18] The Q, F spelling *Pathan* (l. 242) must be a misprint for *Panthean* as used in l. 333 (Q, F).

Occasional F spellings like *Capuchius* H8 4.2.110 and *Venti(d)gius* TmA 1.2.9, 3.3.3, 8 point to [tʃ] in the former and [dʒ] in the latter. Also, in those days the Greek ending *-es* was pronounced [e:z].

In the pronunciation of Italian names we observe the practice of rendering stressed Italian [a:] by English [ɑ:] in names like *Bassanio, Gonzago, Montano, Bellario, Cesario,* etc.; indeed, this vowel is virtually the only Italian coloring given to the names in question. Since Shakespeare's spelling is at times phonetic (cf. *Capuchius, Ventidgius* above), Italian [t:ʃ][19] appears as English *ch* in *Petruchio* and *Borachio,* which should therefore be pronounced [piˈtru:tʃ(j)ou, -iou] and [bouˈrɑ:tʃiou] and not with [-kiou] as is often erroneously done. The treatment of the initial *I* in *Iachimo* and *Iago* is strangely inconsistent. In both, *I* represents *J*: *Iachimo* is a variant spelling of Italian *Giachimo* or *Giacomo, Iago* is Spanish *Jago* or *Iago* (as in *Santiago*). The fact that *Iachimo* is always trisyllabic in Shakespeare favors the modern spelling *Jachimo* and the pronunciation [ˈdʒækimou] with the possible variant [ˈdʒɑ:kimou]; the regular British form [aiˈækimou] is metrically and phonologically unsatisfactory. *Iago,* on the other hand, which should be

[18] Bailey's *Dictionary* of 1728 indicates the stress on the first syllable (OED).

[19] *Petruchio* and *Borachio* contain the Italian suffixes *-uccio* and *-accio.*

['jɑːgou][20] or ['dʒeigou], is always trisyllabic in Shakespeare (except at O 5.2.154), a circumstance suggesting
that Shakespeare himself used to pronounce its initial *I*
as [i], which may easily have become [j] at O 5.2.154,
where the name is disyllabic. For *Stephano*, which is
normally stressed ⏑́ ⏑ ⏑, the meter may seem to
indicate the accentuation ⏑ ⏑́ ⏑ (and the consequent
pronunciation [ste'fɑːnou]) at MV 5.1.28, 51, but neither
line becomes rhythmically unmanageable by the retention
of the normal stress ⏑́ ⏑ ⏑.

French Names

French names are treated even more erratically in English
than Italian ones. Some have become fully anglicized but
others only partially so—compare e.g. *Paris* and *Anjou*,
Agincourt and *Gerard*. In Shakespeare's day anglicization
had no doubt gone much further, as may be inferred from
occasional spellings and the scansion of certain lines. Thus
Chatillon, spelled *Chatillion* J 1.1.1, 50, etc. and always
stressed ⏑ ⏑́ ⏑, cannot have had the modern French
pronunciation [ʃatijõ] but was probably pronounced
[ʃə'til(j)on] or [ʃæ'til(j)ən]; some such form should therefore be used today so as to retain the rhythm of the
pentameter line. Spellings like *Callis* (Calais), *Marcellus*
(Marseilles), *Grand Pree* and *Grand Prie* (Grandpré),
Lavatch (Lavache) and *Foyes* (Foix) corroborate this

---

[20] According to Professor Harold Orton, this is now the general
pronunciation, though it does not as yet appear in any pronouncing
dictionary.

natural tendency in the language. So does Pistol's *Signieur Dew* (Seigneur Dieu), which itself suggests the pronunciation [fju:] for the second syllable of *Lafeu*, whose *La-* probably stands for [lə] (*le*). Nevertheless, 16th-century French pronunciation was not exactly the same as today in all instances. As late as 1530 John Palsgrave recommended the use of [ɔi] for French *oi*, though this by the end of the century had become [wɛ] when final;[21] perhaps a diphthong of this type or the like will explain the inverted spelling *Poictiers* for *Pathay* 1H6 4.1.19. In any case, Shakespeare's rhyme *destroy*: *pardonne moy* R2 5.3.119–20, as well as Pistol's misunderstanding of French *moi* as *moy* H5 4.4.12, 23, permits us to postulate [ɔi] for his period in all French names ending in *oy, ois,* or *oix*. Even at the beginning of the 17th century some French grammarians insisted on the pronunciation of the final consonant in *-ois* and *-oix*, a fact that will explain the [z] not only in *Amiens, Marseilles,* but also in *Artois, Blois, Bois,* and others; the Elizabethans may have used it also in *Chartreux,* whereas *Bordeaux* appears to have had a vulgar pronunciation ['bə:rdəks]. The scansion of the line "O Lymoges, O Austria, thou dost shame" (J 3.1.114) is very troublesome unless we assume that Shakespeare pronounced *Lymoges* as a trisyllable ['limo:dʒis], in which case we obtain a pentameter line with a "tumbling" caesura in the fourth foot: "Áus|tria, ‖ thóu|"; the alternative would be a headless line with the first two metrical stresses on "Ó Lymóges" and *Lymoges* pronounced either [li'mo:ʒ] or [li'mo:dʒis] (today [li'mouʒ] or [li'moudʒis]). Finally

[21] A. Ewert, *The French Language* (London, 1933), p. 62.

we may note that the modern form *Bretagne* occurs nowhere in Shakespeare; instead we find in F *Britaine* and *Britaigne* (always disyllabic) as well as *Brittanie* (3H6 4.6.97, 101, trisyllabic). Since *Britai(g)ne* was pronounced ['britən], modernization to *Bretagne* or *Britanny* cannot fail to violate the rhythm.

SHAKESPEARE'S NAMES

Aaron   ˈɛərən, *S* ˈɛːrən

Abel   ˈeibl̩

Abergavenny   ˌæbərgəˈveni, ˌæbərˈgeni
> The second variant should be used H8 1.1.211,
> 1.2.137 as shown by the scansion and the F spelling
> *Aburgany.*

Abhorson   əbˈhɔːrsən

Abraham   ˈeibrəhæm, ˈeibrəm, *S* ˈeːbrəhæm, ˈeːbrəm
> The disyllabic form should be used R3 4.3.38, MV
> 1.3.73 (spelled *Abram* in the latter instance).

Absyrtus   əbˈsəːrtəs

Academe   ˌækəˈdiːm

Acheron   ˈækərɔn, -rən

Achilles   əˈkiliːz, *S* əˈkileːz

Achitophel   əˈkitəˌfel

Actaeon æk'ti:ən, *S* æk'te:ən

Actium 'æktiəm, 'ækʃiəm, 'ækʃjəm
Disyllabic AC 3.7.52.

Adallas ə'dæləs

Adam 'ædəm

Adonis ə'dounis, *S* ə'do:nis

Adrian 'eidriən, *S* 'e:driən

Adriana ˌeidri'ɑ:nə, -'ænə, -'einə, *S* ˌe:dri'æ(:)nə

Adriano de Armado ˌeidri'ɑ:nou də ɑ:r'mɑ:dou, *Sp* aðri'ano ðe ar'maðo

Adriatic ˌeidri'ætik

Aeacida, –des i:'æsidə, -di:z, *S* e:'æside:, -de:z, *L* ai'akida, -de̦:s

Aegeon i:'dʒi(:)ən, *S* e:'dʒi:ən

Aegle 'i:gli:, *S* 'e:gli

Aemilia i(:)'miliə, -ljə, *S* e(:)'miliə, -ljə

Aemilius i(:)'miliəs, -ljəs, *S* e(:)'miljəs

Aeneas i(:)'ni(:)æs, -əs, *S* e(:)'ne:æs

Aeolus 'i(:)oləs, -ələs, *S* 'e:ələs
Perhaps disyllabic ['i:ləs] 2H6 3.2.92.

Aesculapius ˌi:skju'leipjəs, -piəs, *A* ˌeskjə'leipiəs. *S* ˌe(:)skə'le:pjəs

Aeson 'i:sɔn, *S* 'e:sɔn

Aesop 'i:sɔp, *S* 'e:sɔp

Aetna 'etnə

Afric 'æfrik

Africa 'æfrikə, *S* + 'æfrike:

Agamemnon ˌægə'memnən, -nɔn

Agenor ə'dʒi:nɔ:r

Agincourt 'ædʒinkɔ:rt

Agrippa ə'gripə

Aguecheek 'eigju̧tʃi:k, *S* 'e:gi̧tʃi:k

28

Ajax 'eidʒæks, *S* 'e:dʒe:ks, 'e:dʒæks

The pun *Ajax–a jakes* LLL 5.2.579–81 favors the former S variant, as does the fact that the second *a* in *Ajax* was originally long (L *Aiāx*); see *Sh.Pr.*, p. 177.

Alanson, see *Alençon*

Alarbus ə'lɑːrbəs

Alban 'ɔ(ː)lbən

Albany 'ɔ(ː)lbəni, 'ælbəni

Probably disyllabic ['ɔːlbni] L 1.1.67.

Albion 'ælbjən, -iən, *S* 'ælbjən, -iɔn

Trisyllabic H5 3.5.14, 3H6 3.3.49, L 3.2.91.

Alcibiades ˌælsi'baiədiːz, *S* ˌælsi'bəi(ə)deːz

Probably four syllables TmA 1.1.250, 5.1.206.

Alcides æl'saidiːz, *S* æl'səideːz

Alecto ə'lektou

Alençon ə'lensən, -sɔn, *Fr* alɑ̃sɔ̃

The F spelling *Alanson* points to S [ə'lænsən].

Aleppo ə'lepou

Alexander ˌælig'zɑːndər, -'zæn-, *S* ˌælig'zæ(ː)ndər

Alisander LLL 5.2.567 etc. represents a variant without [g] which survived into the 18th century.

Alexandria ˌælig'zɑːndriə, -'zæn-, *S* ˌælig'zæ(ː)ndrieː

Alexas ə'leksəs

Alice 'ælis, *S+* æls

Spelled *Alce* TS pr.2.112; see *Sh.Pr.*, p. 285.

Aliena ˌeili'iːnə

Alonso ə'lɔnzou

Alphonso æl'fɔnzou, -sou

Althaea æl'θiːə, *S* æl'θeːə

Alton 'ɔːltən

Ama(i)mon ə'meimɔn, *S* ə'meːmɔn

America ə'merikə, *S* + ə'merike:

Amiens æmiənz, *S* 'æmjənz, *Fr* amjɛ̃

Amphimachus æm'fiməkəs

Ampthill 'æmtəl

Amurath (see p. 6) ˌɑmu'rɑt, 'æmuˌræt

Amyntas ə'mintəs

Anchises æn'kaisi:z, æŋ-, *S* æn'kəise:z

Ancus 'æŋkəs

Andren 'ændrən

Andrew 'ændru:

Andromache æn'drɔməki
   Apparently trisyllabic TC 5.3.84, with mute final *e*.

Andronicus, –i (see p. 20) æn'drɔnikəs, -isai, *S* -isəi

Angelica æn'dʒelikə, *S* æn'dʒelike:

Angelo 'ændʒilou

Angiers 'ændʒiərz, *S* + æn'dʒi:rz
   Stressed __ ⏌ J 2.1.1.

Angus 'æŋgəs

Anjou 'ændʒu:, ɑ̃:ŋ'ʒu:, *S* 'ændʒu:, æn'dʒu:, *Fr* ɑ̃ʒu
   Stressed __ ⏌ 1H6 5.3.95, 2H6 4.1.86.

Anna 'ænə

Anne æn

Anselme 'ænselm

Antenor æn'ti:nɔ:*r*, -nə*r*

Antenorides ˌænti'nɔridi:z, *S* -de:z

Anthonio, see *Antonio*

Anthony 'æntəni, 'ænθəni, *S* 'æntəni

Antiates 'ænʃieits, *S* 'ænʃie:ts
   Apparently disyllabic C 1.6.59, unless the line is an
   alexandrine.

Antigonus æn'tigənəs

Antioch 'æntiɔk, -tjɔk

30

Antiochus æn'taiəkəs, *S* æn'təi(ə)kəs
Trisyllabic P 1.3.20, 3.pr.25.
Antiopa æn'taiəpə, *S* æn'təiəpe:
Antipholus an'tifələs
Antium 'ænʃiəm, *S* 'ænʃəm
Antoniad æn'touniæd
Antonio æn'touniou, -njou
Antonius æn'touniəs, -njəs
Antony, see *Anthony*
Apemantus ˌæpi'mæntəs, -pə-
Apollo ə'pɔlou
Apollodorus əˌpɔlə'dɔ:rəs
Aquilon 'ækwilɔn
Aquitaine ˌækwi'tein, *S* ˌækwi'te:n
Arabia ə'reibjə, -biə, *S* ə're:bjə, -bie:
Aragon 'ærəgən
Arc ɑ:rk
Arcas 'ɑ:rkəs
Archelaus ˌɑ:rki'leiəs, *S* ˌɑ:rki'le:əs
Archibald 'ɑ:rtʃiˌbɔ:ld, -bəld
Archidamus ˌɑ:rki'deiməs, *S* ˌɑ:rki'de:məs
Arcite 'ɑ:rsait, *S* 'ɑ:rsəit
Arde (*Ardres*) ɑ:rd
Ardea 'ɑ:rdiə, *S* 'ɑ:rdjə
Arden 'ɑ:rdn̩
Argier ɑ:r'dʒiər, *S* ɑ:r'dʒi:r
Argus 'ɑ:rgəs
Ariachne ˌæri'ækni
Ariadne ˌæri'ædni
Ariel 'ɛəriəl, *A* + 'eiriəl, 'ær-, *S* 'ɛ:riəl, -rjəl
Aries 'ɛər(i)i:z, 'ær(i)i:z, *S* 'ɛ:r(j)e:z
Arion ə'raiən, *S* ə'rəiən

31

Aristotle ˈærɪstɔtl̩, *A* ˈærəˌstɔtl̩

Armado, see *Adriano de Armado*

Armagnac ˈɑːrmənˌjæk, *Fr* armaɲak

Armenia ɑːrˈmiːnɪə, -njə, *S* ɑːrˈmɪnjə, -niːe:

Artemidorus ˌɑːrtəmiˈdɔːrəs

Artesius ɑːrˈtiːʒəs, -zjəs

Arthur ˈɑːrθər, *S* ɑːrtər

Artois ɑːrˈtwɑː, *S* a(ː)rˈtɔiz, *Fr* artwa

Arundel ˈærəndl̩

Arviragus ɑːrˈvirəgəs, *S* ˌɑːrviˈreːgəs
　　Stressed ⌣ — — ⌣ — Cy 3.3.96, 5.5.359.

Asaph ˈæsəf, ˈæzəf, ˈeisəf

Ascanius æsˈkeiniəs, -njəs

Asher House ˈæʃər ˈhaus, *S* ˈæʃər ˈhəus

Ashford ˈæʃfərd

Asia ˈeiʃə, *A* + ˈeiʒə, *S* ˈeːʃə, ˈeːʃie:
　　Trisyllabic AC 1.2.105, CE 1.1.134, 2H4 2.4.178
　　(where it rhymes with *day* and hence should end in
　　[-iei])—see p. 18, n. 13.

Asmath ˈæzməθ

Assyrian əˈsiriən, *S* əˈsirjən

Astraea æsˈtriːə, *S* æsˈtreːə

Atalanta ˌætəˈlæntə

Ate ˈeiti, ˈɑːti, *S* ˈeːti

Athens ˈæθinz

Athol ˈæθəl

Atlas ˈætləs

Atropos ˈætropɔs, -trə-

Aubrey ˈɔːbri

Audrey ˈɔːdri

Aufidius ɔːˈfidiəs, *S* + ɔːˈfidjəs

August ˈɔːgəst

32

Augustus ɔːˈɡʌstəs

Aulis ˈɔːlis

Aumerle ɔːˈməːrl

Aurora ɔːˈrɔːrə, *S* ɔːˈrɔːrə

Austria ˈɔːstriə, *S* + ˈɔːstrie:

Autolycus ɔːˈtɔlikəs

Auvergne ouˈvɛərn, -ˈvəːrn, *S* ɔːˈvɛːrn, *Fr* oˈvɛrɲ

Babylon ˈbæbilən

Bacchus ˈbækəs

Bagot ˈbæɡət

Bajazet ˌbædʒəˈzet

Balthazar ˌbælθəˈzaːr, bælˈθæzər

    Stressed ⏜ — ⏜ CE 5.1.223, RJ 5.1.12, perhaps
    — ⏜ — CE 3.1.19, 22.

Banbury ˈbænbəri

Bangor ˈbæŋɡər, *A* + ˈbæŋɡɔːr

Banister ˈbænistər

Banquo ˈbæŋkwou

Baptista bæpˈtistə

Bar baːr

Barabbas ˈbærəbəs, -bæs

    The scansion and the F spelling *Barrabas* MV
    4.1.296 show this to be the S pronunciation, not
    [bəˈræbəs], which is invariable today in British and
    American English.

Barbara ˈbaːrbərə, -brə, *S* ˈbaːrbəri, -bri

    The F spelling *Barbarie* O 4.3.26, 33 reflects the
    popular form of the name in the 16th century.

Barbary ˈbaːrbəri

Barbason ˈbaːrbəsən

Bardolph ˈbɑːrdɔlf, *S* ˈbaːrdɔlf, ˈbaːrdl̩

Spelled *Bardol* 1H4 2.4.329.

Bargulus ˈbɑːrgjuləs, *S* ˈbaːrgələs

Barkloughly bɑːrkˈlouli, *S* baːrkˈloːli

Holinshed's *Barclowlie,* which S took over, is an error for *Hertlowli,* now *Harlech* in North Wales.

Barnardine ˈbɑːrnərˌdiːn, *S* ˈbaːrnərˌdiːn

Possibly stressed — ⫠ — MM 4.2.68.

Barnes bɑːrnz

Barnet ˈbɑːrnit

Barson ˈbɑːrsn̩

Barson 2H4 5.3.94 is probably to be identified with *Barston,* Warwickshire, for which see *PN Wa*, p. 55.

Bartholomew bɑːrˈθɔləmjuː, *S* ˈbaːrtəlmjuː

Spelled *Bartholmew* TS pr.1.105, where clearly stressed ⫠ — ⫡.

Basan ˈbeisæn

Basilisco ˌbæziˈliskou

Basimecu ˌbæziməˈkjuː, ˌbei-

Rendered *bus mine cue* 2H6 4.7.31 Q, for which see *Sh.Pr.*, pp. 69 f.

Basingstoke ˈbeiziŋstouk, *S* ˈbeːzinstoːk

Bassanio bəˈsɑːniou, -njou

It is impossible to determine whether the second *a* was [aː], [æː], or [eː] in S, where the name is always trisyllabic.

Basset ˈbæsit

Bassianus ˌbæsiˈeinəs

Bates beits

Baynard's Castle ˈbeinərdz ˈkɑːsl̩, *A*, *S* ˈkæ(ː)sl̩

Bayonne beiˈɔn, *S* beːˈɔn, *Fr* bajɔn

Bead biːd, *S* beːd

Beatrice ˈbiətris, *S*+ ˈbiːtris, ˈbetris

Disyllabic *Beatrice* MA 3.1.21, 24, 37, 43 may have had [iː] or [e] in the first syllable; see *Sh.Pr.*, p. 287.

Beau, see *Le Beau*

Beaufort ˈboufərt, *S* ˈboːfərt, -fərd

Consistently spelled *Beauford* in F.

Beaumond ˈboumənd

Beaumont ˈboumənt, -mɔnt

Perhaps stressed ‿ ⏊ H5 3.5.44, 4.8.105.

Bedford ˈbedfərd

Bedlam ˈbedləm

Beelzebub bi(ː)ˈelzibʌb, *S* ˈbelzibʌb

Spelled *Belzebub* M 2.3.4, TN 5.1.291.

Bel beil, *S* beːl

Belarius (see p. 6) bəˈlɛəriəs, be-, *A*+ -ˈlær-, -ˈleir-, *S* bəˈlɛːrjəs

Belch beltʃ

Belgia ˈbeldʒiə, *S*+ ˈbeldʒieː

Bellario (see p. 6) beˈlɑːriou, bə-, -rjou, -ˈlɛər-

Bellona bəˈlounə, be-

Belman ˈbelmən

Belmont ˈbelmɔnt, -mənt

Benedick ˈbenidik

Benedictus ˌbeniˈdiktəs

Bennet ˈbenit

Bentii ˈbenʃiai, *S* ˈbenʃiəi

Bentivolii ˌbentiˈvouliai, *S* -ˈvoːliəi

Benvolio benˈvouliou, -ljou

Bergamo ˈbəːrgəmou, *S* ˈbəːrgəmoː, ˈbaːr-

Bergomask ˈbəːrgəmɑːsk, *A*, *S* -mæ(ː)sk

Spelled *Burgomaske* MND 5.1.368, for which see *Sh.Pr.*, p. 252.

Berkeley ˈbɑːrkli, *A* ˈbəːrkli, *S* ˈbɑːrkli

Bermoothes bərˈmuːðəz

> *Bermoothes* T 1.2.229 is clearly a phonetic rendering of Sp *Bermudez*.

Bernardo bərˈnɑːrdou

Berowne, see *Biron*

Berry ˈberi

Bertram ˈbəːrtrəm, *S* + ˈbɑːrtrəm

Berwick ˈberik

> The F spellings *Barwick(e)* 2H6 2.1.83, 159, 3H6 2.5.128 may indicate a pronunciation [ˈbærik] or [ˈbarik].

Bess bes

Bessy ˈbesi

Best best

Bevis ˈbevis, ˈbiːvis

Bezonian biˈzounjən, -niən

Bianca biˈæŋkə, *S* + biˈæŋkeː, ˈbjæŋkə

> Disyllabic TS 2.1.346.

Bigot ˈbigət

Biondello ˌbi(ː)ənˈdelou

Birnam ˈbəːrnəm

Biron biˈruːn

> Spelled *Berowne* Q, F and rhyming with *moone* LLL 4.3.230–2.

Blackfriars ˈblækˈfrai̯ərz, *S* -ˈfrai̯(ə)rz

Blackheath ˈblækˈhiːθ, *S* -ˈhe(ː)θ

Blackmere ˈblækmiər, *S* -miːr, -mər

Blanc, see *Port le Blanc*

Blanch blɑːntʃ, *A*, *S* blæ(ː)ntʃ

Blithild ˈbliðild, ˈbliθild

Blois blwɑː, *S* blɔiz, *Fr* blwa

36

Blount, see *Blunt*

Blumer, see *Bulmer*

Blunt blʌnt

Boar's Head ˈbɔː*r*z ˈhed, *S* ˈboːrz ˈ*h*ed, ˈ*h*id

Bocchus ˈbɔkəs

Bohemia (see p. 13) bo*u*ˈhiːmjə, *S* bo(ː)ˈ*h*iːmjə

Bohun buːn

Bois bɔiz, *Fr* bwa

Bolingbroke ˈbɔliŋbruk, ˈbuliŋbruk, *S* ˈbulinbruk
Spelled *Bullingbrook(e)*, *Bullinbrook(e)* R2 1.1.124, 2.2.60, 62, etc.

Bona ˈbounə

Bonville ˈbɔnvil

Borachio (see p. 22) bo*u*ˈrɑːtʃiou, *S* bo(ː)ˈraːtʃioː, boˈrætʃioː

Bordeaux bɔː*r*ˈdou, *Fr* bɔrdo
Spelled *Burde(a)ux* and always stressed ⏊ — in S. The popular (vulgar) pronunciation may have been [ˈbəːrdəks]; see *Sh.Pr.*, p. 338, n. 1.

Boreas ˈbɔ(ː)riæs

Bosworth Field ˈbɔzwə(ː)*r*θ ˈfiːld

Bottom ˈbɔtəm

Bouciqualt ˈbuːsikɔːlt, *Fr* busiko

Boult boult

Bourbon ˈbuə*r*bən, -bɔn, *Fr* burbɔ̃

Bourchier ˈbautʃə*r*, *S* ˈbəutʃər

Bourgogne (see also *Burgundy*) *Fr* burgɔɲ

Boyet bɔiˈet, *Fr* bwajɛ

Brabant brəˈbænt, *S* ˈbræbənt
Always stressed ⏊ — in S.

Brabantio brəˈbænʃou

Brabbler ˈbræblə*r*

Bracy ˈbreisi

Brain(e)ford, see *Brentford*

Brakenbury ˈbrækənbəri

Brandon ˈbrændən

Brecknock ˈbreknək

Brentford ˈbrentfərd, S ˈbreːnfərd

> Always spelled *Brain(e)ford* in S, and still pronounced [ˈbreinfəd] locally.

Bretagne (see also *Britaigne*) *Fr* brətaɲ

> This modern form occurs nowhere in S; see p. 25.

Breton ˈbretən, S ˈbritən

> Always spelled *Brit(t)aine* in S (R3 4.3.40, 4.4.523, 5.3.317, 333).

Briareus braiˈɛəriəs, S brəiˈɛːriəs

Bridgenorth ˈbridʒnɔːrθ

Bridget ˈbridʒit

Bristol ˈbristl̩, S + ˈbristoː

> The F spelling *Bristow* represents the old form of the name.

Britai(g)ne (*Bretagne*) ˈbritən, ˈbritn̩

> This is the regular F spelling; see p. 25.

Britain ˈbritən, ˈbritn̩

Briton ˈbritən, ˈbritn̩

Brittany ˈbritəni

> Appears only 3H6 2.6.97, 4.6.97, 101.

Brocas ˈbrɔkəs, ˈbroukəs, S ˈbrɔkəs

> Spelled *Broccas* R2 5.6.14; see p. 7.

Brook bruk

Brundusium brʌnˈdjuːʒiəm, -ziəm, A + -ˈduː-

Brutus ˈbrutəs

> The vocative *Brute* JC 3.1.77 is [ˈbruːti] or [ˈbruːte].

Buckingham ˈbʌkiŋəm, A ˈbʌkiŋˌhæm, S ˈbʌkinəm

Bucklersbury ˈbʌklərzbəri

Bull bul

Bullcalf ˈbulˌkɑːf, *A*, *S* -ˌkæ(ː)f

Bullen ˈbulin

Bullingbroke, see *Bolingbroke*

Bulmer ˈbulmər

Burgh bəːrg

Burgundy ˈbəːrgəndi, *S* ˈbəːrgən(d)i

    Spelled *Burgundy*, *Burgonie* (9×) and *Burgogne*
    H5 5.2.7, but always trisyllabic.

Burton ˈbəːrtṇ

Burton-heath ˈbəːrtṇ ˈhiːθ, *S* ˈheːθ

Bury St. Edmunds ˈberi sṇtˈedməndz, *A* seint

Bushy ˈbuʃi

Butcher ˈbutʃər

Butler ˈbʌtlər

Butts bʌts

Byzantium baiˈzæntiəm, bi-, -nʃiəm

Cade keid, *S* keːd

Cadmus ˈkædməs

Cadwal ˈkædwɔːl

Cadwallader kædˈwɔ(ː)lədər

Caelius ˈsiːljəs, -iəs, *S* ˈseːljəs

Caesar ˈsiːzər, *S* ˈseːzər

Caesarion si(ː)ˈzɛəriən, *S* se(ː)ˈzɛːrjən

Cain kein, *S* keːn

Caithness ˈkeiθnes

Caius (Roman name; see p. 20) ˈkaiəs, *A* ˈkeiəs, *S*
    ˈkeːəs

Caius (Dr., MWW; see p. 20) ki:z, *S* ke:z

Calaber 'kælǝbǝr

Calais 'kælei, 'kæli(s), *S* 'kælis, *Fr* kalɛ
    Spelled *Callis, Callice* e.g. J 3.3.73, R2 1.1.126.

Calchas 'kælkǝs

Caliban 'kælibæn, -bǝn

Calipolis kǝ'lipǝlis

Calpurnia kæl'pǝ:*r*niǝ, -njǝ
    Invariably spelled *Calphurnia* in S.

Calydon 'kælidǝn, -dɔn

Cambio 'kæmbiou, -bjou

Cambria 'kæmbriǝ

Cambridge 'keimbridʒ

Cambyses kæm'baisi:z, *S* kæm'bǝise:z

Camelot 'kæmilɔt

Camillo kǝ'milou

Campeius kæm'pi:ǝs, *S* kæm'pe:ǝs

Candy 'kændi

Canidius kǝ'nidiǝs, *S*+ kǝ'nidjǝs

Canon Street 'kænǝn 'stri:t

Canterbury 'kæntǝrbǝri, -bri, -beri, *A*+ -ˌberi

Capaneus ˌkæpǝ'ni:ǝs

Capel (see also *Capulet* and p. 7) 'kæpļ

Caper 'keipǝr

Capet 'keipit, 'kæpit, *S* 'kæpit, *Fr* kapɛ

Caphis 'keifis

Capilet 'kæpilit, -lǝt

Capitol 'kæpitļ

Cappadocia ˌkæpǝ'dousiǝ, -sjǝ, -ʃǝ, *S* ˌkæpǝ'do:ʃǝ

Capucius (see p. 22) kǝ'pju:ʃǝs, *S* kǝ'pju:tʃǝs

Capulet 'kæpjulit, 'kæpjǝlǝt, *S* 'kæpilit, -ǝlet
    See further *Sh.Pr.*, p. 282.

Car kɑːr

Carlisle kɑːrˈlail, S kaːrˈləil

Carnarvonshire kərˈnɑːrvənʃiər, -ʃər

Carthage ˈkɑːrθidʒ, S ˈkaːrθidʒ, -tidʒ

Casca ˈkæskə

Cassado kəˈsɑːdou

Cassandra kəˈsændrə

Cassibelan kæˈsibələn

Cassio ˈkæsiou, ˈkæʃ(j)ou

Castor ˈkɑːstər, A, S ˈkæ(ː)stər

Cataian kəˈteiən, S kəˈteːən

Catesby ˈkeitsbi, S ˈkeːtsbi

Trisyllabic R3 3.1.157 and 3.7.83, perhaps to be pronounced [ˈkætizbi].

Catling ˈkætliŋ, S ˈkætlin

Cato ˈkeitou, S ˈkeːto

Caucasus ˈkɔːkəsəs

Cawdor ˈkɔːdər

Cedius ˈsiːdiəs, -djəs

Celia ˈsiːliə, -ljə, S ˈsiːlieː, -ljə

Censorinus ˌsensəˈrainəs, S -ˈrəinəs

Centaur ˈsentɔːr

Cerberus ˈsəːrbərəs, -brəs

Ceres ˈsiəriːz, S ˈseːreːz

Cerimon ˈserimɔn

Cesario səˈzɑːriou, -jou, S səˈzɛːrioː, -ˈzɑːrjoː

Cham kæm

Champagne ʃæmˈpein, S ʃæmˈpeːn, Fr ʃã·paɲ

Charbon ˈʃɑːrbɔn, S ˈʃaːrbɔn

Charing Cross ˈtʃæriŋ, ˈtʃɛəriŋ, ˈkrɔs, A + ˈkrɔːs

Charlemain ˈʃɑːrləˈmein, A -ˌmein

Charles tʃɑːrlz

41

Charmian 'kɑːɾmiən, -mjən, 'tʃɑːɾ-

Charolois (*Charolais*) 'ʃærələɔiz, *Fr* ʃarolɛ

Charon 'kɛərən, *S* 'kɛːɾən

Chartham (in Kent) 'tʃɑːɾtəm, *S* 'tʃɑːɾtəm
> F (2H6 4.2.92) has *Chartam*, but Q has *Chattam*
> (also SD), which most eds. identify with *Chatham*;
> see, however, Arden Ed., p. 112.

Chartreux ʃɑːɾ'trə:, *S* 'ʃɑːɾtruː(z), *Fr* ʃartrø
> Stressed ⏑ — in S.

Charybdis kə'ribdis

Chatham 'tʃætəm, *A* + 'tʃæðæm

Chatillon *S* ʃə'til(j)ɔn, ʃæ'tilən, -ljən, *Fr* ʃatijɔ̃
> Always stressed — ⏑ — in S; see p. 23.

Cheapside 'tʃiːp'said, *S* 'tʃeːp'səid

Chertsey 'tʃəːɾtsi, *S* 'tʃɑːɾtsi

Chester 'tʃestəɾ

Chetas (see p. 7) 'kiːtəs

Childeric 'tʃildərik

Chiron 'kaiərɔn, -ən, *S* 'kəirən

Chitopher 'tʃitəfəɾ, 'kit-

Christopher 'kristəfəɾ

Christophero kris'tɔfərou

Chus (see p. 7) kʌs, kus

Cicely 'sisəli, *S* 'sisli
> Disyllabic CE 3.1.31, TS pr.2.91.

Cicero 'sisərou

Ciceter (now *Cirencester*) 'sisitəɾ

Cilicia sai'liʃiə, si'liʃjə, -siə, -sjə, *S* səi'liʃ(j)ə

Cimber 'simbəɾ

Cimmerian si'miəriən

Cinna 'sinə

Cinque–ports 'siŋk'pɔːɾts

42

Circe   ˈsəːrsi(ː)

Clare   klɛər, *S* klɛːr

Clarence   ˈklærəns

Claribel   ˈklærəˌbel, -ri-

Claudio   ˈklɔːdiou, -djou

Claudius   ˈklɔːdiəs, -djəs

Cleitus   ˈklaitəs, *S* ˈkləitəs

     Spelled *Clytus* H5 4.7.41, 48.

Clement   ˈklemənt

Cleomenes   kli(ː)ˈɔminiːz, *S* -neːz

Cleon   ˈkliːɔn

Cleopatra   klioˈpɑːtrə, kliə-, -ˈpætrə, -ˈpeitrə, *S* -ˈpeːtrə,
     -ˈpætrə

Clifford   ˈklifərd

Clifton   ˈkliftən, -tņ

Clitus   ˈklaitəs, *S* ˈkləitəs

Cloten   ˈkloutņ, *S* ˈklɔtņ

     Spelled *Clotten* Cy 3.4.136; see also *Sh.Pr.*, p. 71.

Clothair   ˈkloutɛər, -θɛər, *S* ˈklɔːtɛːr, -θɛːr

Clotharius   klouˈtɛəriəs, -jəs, -ˈθɛər-, *S* klɔ(ː)ˈtɛːrjəs,
     -ˈθɛːrjəs

Clowder   ˈklaudər, *S* ˈkləudər

Cneius (or *Gnaeus*)   ˈniːəs, *S* ˈneːəs

Cnidus   ˈnaidəs, *S* ˈnəidəs

Cobham   ˈkɔbəm

Cobweb   ˈkɔbweb

Cocytus   kouˈsaitəs, *S* kɔ(ː)ˈsəitəs

Coeur de Lion   ˌkəːrdəˈliːʒːŋ, -ˈliːɔŋ, -ˈliːən, -ˈliːɔn, *Fr*
     kœrdəljõ

Colbrand   ˈkoulbrænd

Colchis   ˈkɔlkis, ˈkɔltʃis

Coldspur   ˈkouldˌspəːr

Colebrook ˈkoulbruk

Coleville ˈkoulvil, *S* ˈkoːl(ə)vil
> Trisyllabic 2H4 4.3.79.

Collatine ˈkɔlətain, *S* -təin

Collatinus ˌkɔləˈtainəs, *S* -ˈtəinəs

Collatium kɔˈleiʃəm, *S* kɔˈleːʃəm

Colmekill ˈkoumkil, *S* ˈkoːmkil

Colossus kəˈlɔsəs

Comagene ˌkɔməˈdʒiːni, *S* ˈkɔmedʒiːn
> The F spelling *Comageat* AC 3.6.74 is probably
> an error for *Comagean* or *Comagena* (as in Plutarch);
> the name seems to be trisyllabic here.

Comfect ˈkʌmfit, ˈkɔm-
> *Comfect* MA 4.1.318 is a fanciful spelling of *comfit*.

Cominius kəˈminjəs, -niəs

Conrade (see p. 5, n. 2) ˈkɔnræd

Constance ˈkɔnstəns

Constantine ˈkɔnstəntain, -tiːn, *S* -təin, -tiːn

Constantinople ˌkɔnstæntiˈnoupl̩

Cophetua kouˈfetjuə, -tʃuə
> Trisyllabic in S, and spelled *Couitha* F, *Couetua* Q,
> 2H4 5.3.106, which point to [v] for *ph* and [ə] for
> *ua*, thus [ko(ː)ˈvetə] or [ko(ː)ˈvi(ː)tə].

Cophil, see *Sutton Coldfield*

Copperspur ˈkɔpərˌspəːr

Corambus kouˈræmbəs, kə-

Cordelia kɔːrˈdiːljə, -liə, *S* -ljə, -lieː
> Always trisyllabic, except possibly at L 5.3.271.

Corin ˈkɔrin, *A* + ˈkɔːrin

Corinth ˈkɔrinθ, *A* + ˈkɔːrinθ

Corinthian kəˈrinθiən

Coriolanus ˌkɔriəˈleinəs, *S* ˌkɔrjəˈleːnəs, ˌkɔriə-

Usually four syllables, except at C 3.1.59, 280, 4.6.13, 132, 5.6.89, where five syllables.

Corioli kə'riəli, *A* kə'raiə₁lai ʻ

Whether three syllables (C 1.8.8, 1.9.76, etc.) or four syllables (C 1.9.82, 5.6.90, etc.), it is always stressed on the second syllable. The regular F spelling *Corioles*, with the sporadic variants *Carioles*, *Coriolus*, *Corialus*, points to S [kə'rəi(ə)ləs].

Cornelia kɔ:*r*'ni:liə, -ljə, *S* -lie:, -ljə

Cornelius kɔ:*r*'ni:ljəs

Cornwall 'kɔ:*r*nwəl, -wɔ:l

Cosmo 'kɔzmou

Costard 'kɔstərd

Cotswold 'kɔtswould, *S* 'kɔtsəl(d)

Spelled *Cotsall* MWW 1.1.192, *Cotshold* R2 2.3.9; see *Sh.Pr.*, pp. 40, 329.

Cotus 'koutəs

Counter-gate 'kauntər₁geit, *S* 'kəuntər₁ge:t

Courtney 'kɔ:rtni, *S*+ 'ko:rtni

Coventry 'kɔvəntri

['kʌvəntri] is a very common spelling pronunciation.

Crab kræb

Cranmer 'krænmər

Crassus 'kræsəs

Creon 'kri(:)ɔn

Cressid 'kresid

Cressida 'kresidə, *S*+ 'kreside:

Cressy (*Crécy*) 'kresi

Crete kri:t

Crispian 'krispiən

Crispianus ₁krispi'einəs

Crispin 'krispin

Cromer 'kroumər

Cromwell 'krɔmwəl, 'krʌm-, -wel

Crosby (Place) 'krɔzbi, 'krɔsbi (pleis), *A* + 'krɔ:z-

Cross krɔs, *A* krɔ:s

Cumberland 'kʌmbərlənd

Cupid 'kju:pid

Curan 'kʌrən, *A* 'kə:rən

Curio 'kjuəriou, *S* 'kju:rio:

Curtal 'kə:rtl̩

Curtis 'kə:rtis

Cut kʌt

Cyclops 'saiklɔps, *S* 'səiklɔps

Cydnus 'sidnəs

Cymbeline 'simbili:n, -bəl-

Cynthia 'sinθjə, -θiə
    Always disyllabic in S.

Cyprus 'saiprəs, *S* 'səiprəs

Cyrus 'saiərəs, *S* 'səirəs

Cytherea ˌsiθə'ri(:)ə

Daedalus 'di:dələs, 'dedələs, *S* 'de(:)dələs

Dagonet 'dægonet, -ənit

Daintry, see *Daventry*

Dalmatian dæl'meiʃiən, *S* dæl'me:ʃiən
    Three syllables Cy 3.1.74, four Cy 3.7.3.

Damascus də'mæskəs

Damon 'deimɔn, -mən, *S* 'de:mɔn

Daniel 'dænjəl, *S* + 'dæniəl, 'dænəl
    Apparently both trisyllabic and disyllabic at MV
    4.1.333; for the variant ['dænəl] see *Sh.Pr.*, pp. 289 f.

Danskers 'dænskərz

Daphne 'dæfni

Dardan 'dɑːrdən

Dardanian dɑːr'deinjən, *S* dɑːr'deːnjən

Dardanius dɑːr'deiniəs, -njəs, *S* dɑːr'deːnjəs

Darius də'raiəs, *S* də'rəiəs

Dartford 'dɑːrtfərd

Datchet-lane 'dætʃit'lein

Datchet-mead 'dætʃit'miːd, *S* -'meːd

Dauphin 'dɔːfin, *S* 'dɔlfin, *Fr* dofɛ̃
    Spelled *Dolphin* 1H6 1.1.92 etc., *Daulphin* J 3.1.311,
    representing an earlier form of the name; see
    Dauphin, OED.

Daventry 'dævəntri, 'deintri, *S* 'deːntri
    Spelled *Daintry* 3H6 5.1.6; see *Sh.Pr.*, p. 326, and
    PN Np, pp. 18 f.

Davy 'deivi

Deborah 'debərə

Decius 'diːʃiəs, -ʃ(j)əs

Deep-vow 'diːpvau, *S* -vəu

Deiphobus di:'ifəbəs

Delabreth ˌdelə'breθ, -'bret

De la Car ˌdelə'kɑːr

De la Pole ˌdelə'poul, *S* ˌdelə'puːl
    See further *Sh.Pr.*, pp. 135 f.

Delay di'lei

Delphos 'delfəs

Demetrius di'miːtriəs

Denmark 'denmɑːrk

Dennis 'denis

Denny 'deni

Derby 'dɑːrbi, *A* 'dəːrbi, *S* 'dɑːrbi

Dercetas də'rsitəs, *S* də(ː)r'siːtəs
    Probably stressed — ⸣ — AC 5.1.5; see p. 21.

Desdemon(a) ˌdezdiˈmounə, ˈdezdiˌmɔn

Deucalion dju(:)ˈkeiliən, -ljən, *A* + du:-, *S* -ˈke:ljər

Devonshire ˈdevn̩ʃiər, -ʃər

Dian ˈdaiən, *S* ˈdəiən

Diana daiˈænə, *S* dəiˈænə

Dick dik

Dickon ˈdikən

Dicky ˈdiki

Dictynna dikˈtinə

Dido ˈdaidou, *S* ˈdəido:

Dieu (see p. 24) *S* dju:, *Fr* djø

Dighton ˈdaitn̩, *S* ˈdəitn̩

Diomed ˈdaiəmed, -omed, *S* ˈdəiəmed
   Occasionally disyllabic (with loss of the medial [ə]),
   e.g. TC 5.2.137.

Diomede ˈdaiəmi:d, *S* ˈdəiəme:d

Diomedes ˌdaiəˈmi:di:z, *S* ˌdəiəˈme:de:z

Dion ˈdaiən, *S* ˈdəiən

Dionyza ˌdaiəˈnaizə, *S* ˌdəiəˈnəizə

Dis dis

Disdain disˈdein

Dizie ˈdizi

Dobbin ˈdɔbin

Dogberry ˈdɔgberi, *A* ˈdɔgˌberi, -bəri

Doit dɔit, *S* dəit

Dolabella ˌdɔləˈbelə

Doll dɔl

Dolphin ˈdɔlfin

Dombledon ˈdʌmbl̩dən

Domitius doˈmiʃiəs, də-, *S* doˈmiʃəɐ

Donalbain ˈdɔnl̩bein

Doncaster ˈdɔŋkəstər

Dorcas ˈdɔːrkəs, -kæs

Doreus ˈdɔːriəs

Doricles ˈdɔrikliːz, *S* -kleːz

Dorothy ˈdɔreθi, *A* + ˈdɔː-

Dorset ˈdɔːrsit

Dorsetshire ˈdɔːrsitʃiə, -ʃiʳ

Double dʌbl̩

    Dooble 2H4 3.2.45, 58 may indicate a dialectal
    pronunciation [dubl̩].

Douglas ˈdʌgləs

    Apparently trisyllabic [ˈdʌgələs] 1H4 5.2.33.

Dover ˈdouvər

Downs daunz, *S* dəunz

Dowsabel ˈdausəbel, *S* ˈdəusəbel

Dromio ˈdroumiou, -mjou, *S* ˈdroːmioː, -mjoː

Dropheir ˈdrɔpˈɛər

Drum drʌm

Du Champ djuˈ(t)ʃæmp, *A* + du-, *Fr* dyʃɑ̃

Dull dʌl

Dumain dju(ː)ˈmein, *A* + du-, *S* -ˈmeːn

Dumb dʌm

Duncan ˈdʌŋkən

Dunsinane ˌdʌnsiˈnein, *S* ˌdʌnsiˈneːn

    Apparently stressed ͜ ˊ ͜ M 4.1.93.

Dunsmore ˈdʌnzmɔːr

Dunstable ˈdʌnstəbl̩

Eastcheap ˈiːstʃiːp, *S* ˈeːstʃeːp

Echo ˈekou

Eden ˈiːdn̩, *S* + ˈeːdn̩

Edgar ˈedgər

49

Edmund 'edmənd

Edward 'edwərd

Egeon, see *Aegeon*

Egeus i(:)'dʒi(:)əs, *S* e(:)'dʒi:əs

Eglamour 'egləmuər, -moər, -mɔ:*r*

Egypt 'i:dʒipt, *S* 'e:dʒipt

Elbe elb

Elbow 'elbou

Eleanor, Elinor 'elinər, *S* + 'elnər

    The latter variant 2H6 1.3.150, 2.1.169 (both spelled
    Elnor Q), 2.2.38, 2.3.1, 15, 46.

Elephant 'elifənt

Elizabeth i'lizəbəθ

Ellen 'elən

Elsinore ˌelsi'nɔ:*r*, *A* 'elsəˌnɔ:r

Eltham 'eltəm, -θəm, *S* 'eltəm

    The F spelling is *Eltam*, e.g. 1H6 1.1.170.

Ely 'i:li

Elysium i'liziəm, -ʒiəm

Emilia i'miliə, -ljə, *S* e(:)'miljə, -lie:

Emily 'emili

Emmanuel i'mænjuəl

Enceladus en'selədəs

Endymion en'dimiən

England 'iŋglənd

    Perhaps trisyllabic ['iŋgələnd] R2 4.1.17; see p. 18.

Enobarb 'i:nəˌbɑ:*r*b, 'enə-

Enobarbus ˌi:nə'bɑ:*r*bəs, ˌenə-

Ephesian i'fi:ʒiən

Ephesus 'efisəs

Epicurean ˌepikjuə'ri(:)ən

Epicurus ˌepi'kjuərəs

50

Epidamnum ˌepiˈdæmnəm

Epidaurus ˌepiˈdɔ:rəs

Epistrophus iˈpistrəfəs

Ercles ˈə:rkləz, -li:z, *S* ˈə:rkləz, -le:z, ˈa:rkləz

    Bottom's pronunciation of *Hercules* MND 1.2.31.

Erebus ˈeribəs

Ermengare ˈə:rmənˌga:r(d)

    The name (H5 1.2.82) should end in *-ard*, and the
    above form is therefore probably an *e : d* misprint.

Eros ˈiərɔs, ˈerɔs

Erpingham ˈə:rpiŋəm, -ˌhæm, ˈa:rp-, *S* ˈa:rpinəm, -ˌhæm

Escalus ˈeskələs

Escanes ˈeskəˌni:z, *S* ˈeskəˌne:z

Essex ˈesiks

Ethiop ˈi:θiəp, ˈiθjɔp, *S* ˈe:θiəp, -jɔp

Etna ˈetnə

Eton ˈi:tṇ

Euphrates juˈfreiti:z, *S* ˈju:frəte:z

    AC 1.2.105, where it should today be pronounced
    [ˈju:frəti:z].

Euphronius ju(:)ˈfrouniəs, *S* -ˈfro:niəs, -njəs

Euriphile juəˈrifili:

Europa juəˈroupə

Europe ˈjuərəp, *S* ˈju:rəp

Evans ˈevənz

Eve i:v

Exeter ˈeksətər

Exton ˈekstən

Fabian ˈfeibiən

Falstaff ˈfɔ:lsta:f, *A*, *S* ˈfɔ:lstæ(:)f

Fang fæŋ

51

Far, see *La Far*

Fastolfe ˈfæstɔlf

Fauconberg ˈfɔːkənbəːrg, *Fr* fokõbɛr
> The name appears as *Faulconbridge* H5 **3.5.44**, **4.8.104**.

Faulconbridge ˈfɔː(l)kənbridʒ

Faustus ˈfɔːstəs

Feeble fiːbḷ

Fenton ˈfentən

Fer, see *Le Fer*

Ferdinand ˈfəːrdinənd, *A* ˈfəːrdiˌnænd

Ferrara fəˈrɑːrə, *S* fəˈrɑːrə, -ˈrɛːrə, *It* ferˈrɑːra

Ferrers ˈferərz

Feste ˈfesti

Fidele fiˈdiːli

Fife faif

Finsbury ˈfinzbəri, -bri

Fish Street ˈfiʃ ˈstriːt

Fitzwater fitsˈwɔːtər, *A* ˈfitsˌwɔːtər
> The name is a variant of *Fitzwalter*, now usually pronounced with [l].

Flaminius fləˈminiəs

Flanders ˈflɑːndərz, *A, S* ˈflæ(ː)ndərz

Flavina fləˈviːnə

Flavius ˈfleiviəs, -jəs, *S* ˈfleːvjəs

Fleance ˈfliːəns

Fleet fliːt

Fleming ˈflemiŋ, *S* ˈflemin

Flibbertigibbet ˈflibərtiˈdʒibit

Flint Castle ˈflint ˈkɑːsḷ, *A, S* ˈkæ(ː)sḷ

Flora ˈflɔːrə, *S* ˈfloːrə

Florence ˈflɔrəns, *A +* ˈflɔːrəns

Florentine 'flɔrəntain, A 'flɔːrən̩tiːn, S -tiːn
Florentius flɔ(ː)'renʃəs
Florizel 'flɔrizel, A + 'flɔːri̩zel
Fluellen flu(ː)'elin
Flute fluːt
Foix S fɔiz, Fr fwa
    Spelled *Foyes* H5 4.8.104.
Fontibell 'fɔnti̩bel
Ford fɔːrd, S fɔːrd
Forres 'fɔris, A + 'fɔːris
Forrest 'fɔrist, A + 'fɔːrist
Forthright 'fɔːrθrait, S 'fɔːrθrəit
    The F form *Forthlight* MM 4.3.17 is clearly an error.
Fortinbras 'fɔːrtinbræs
Foyes, see *Foix*
France frɑːns, A, S fræ(ː)ns
Frances, Francis 'frɑːnsis, A, S 'fræ(ː)nsis
Francisca fræn'siskə
Francisco fræn'siskou
Frank fræŋk
Frankfort 'fræŋkfərt, -fɔːrt
Frateretto ̩frætə'retou
Frederick 'fred(ə)rik
    Trisyllabic AYL 1.2.245, disyllabic AYL 5.4.160.
Freetown 'friːtaun, S 'friːtəun
Friz friz
Frogmore 'frɔgmɔːr
Froissart 'frɔisɑːrt, Fr frwɑsɑːr
Froth frɔ(ː)θ
Fulvia 'fʌlviə, -vjə
Furnival 'fəːrnivəl
Fury 'fjuəri

Gabriel ˈgeibriəl, *S* ˈgeːbrəl

Spelled *Gabrel* TS 4.1.136; see *Sh.Pr.*, p. 289.

Gadshill ˈgædzhil, *A* ˈgædzˌhil

Galathe ˈgæləθi(ː)

Galen ˈgeilin, -ən, *S* ˈgeːlən

Gallia ˈgæliə, *S*+ ˈgæljə

Mainly disyllabic in S.

Gallian ˈgæliən, *S* ˈgæljən

Galloway ˈgælowei

Gallus ˈgæləs

Gam gæm

Ganymede ˈgænimiːd, *S*+ ˈgænimed

The F spelling *Ganimed* AYL (8×) may indicate the latter variant.

Gardiner ˈgɑːrdnər

Gargantua gɑːrˈgæntjuə, -tʃuə

Gargrave ˈgɑːrgreiv

Garter Inn ˈgɑːrtər ˈin

Gascony ˈgæskəni

Gaul gɔːl

Gaultier ˈgoutjər, *S* ˈgoːtjər, *Fr* goˑtjẹ

Gaultree ˈgɔː(l)triː(ː)

This is the forest of *Galtres* (spelled *Gualtree* 2H4 4.1.2) in Yorkshire, locally pronounced [ˈgɔːtriz].

Gaunt gɔːnt

Gawsey ˈgɔːzi, ˈgɔːsi

Genoa ˈdʒenouə, *S*+ ˈdʒenoweː

Geoffrey ˈdʒefri

George dʒɔːrdʒ, *S*+ dʒɑːrdʒ

Gerard ˈdʒerɑːrd, ˈdʒerəd, dʒeˈrɑːrd, *S* -rɑːrd, *Fr* ʒerɑːr

Germany ˈdʒəːrməni, *S*+ ˈdʒɑːrməni

54

Gertrude ˈgəːrtruːd

>The regular Q1 spelling *Gertred* may indicate a pronunciation [ˈgəːrtrəd] or [ˈgaːrtrəd], and so probably do the Q2 spellings *Gertra(r)d*.

Gilbert ˈgilbərt

Gilliams ˈgiljəmz

Gillian ˈdʒiliən, -ljən, ˈgil-

Ginn dʒin

Giraldo dʒiˈrældou

Glamis glɑːmz, *S* + ˈglamis

>The name is disyllabic M 1.5.16, 55, 2.2.42, 3.1.1, but may be either monosyllabic or disyllabic elsewhere in M.

Glansdale ˈglænzdeil, -dl̩

Glendower ˈglendauər, glenˈdauər, *S* -dəur, -doːr

>Disyllabic and stressed ‿ — R2 3.1.43 (spelled *Glendor* Q), 1H4 1.3.117, 295, 3.1.78, 87, 4.4.16, 5.5.40, 2H6 2.2.41; trisyllabic and stressed ‿ — ‿ 1H4 3.1.3; otherwise disyllabic in verse and stressed — ‿.

Gloucester ˈglɔstər, *A* + ˈgloːstər

Gloucestershire ˈglɔstərʃər, -ʃiər, *A* + ˈglɔːs-

Gnaeus, see *Cneius*

Gobbo ˈgɔbou

Goffe gɔf, *A* gɔːf, *S* gɔ(ː)f

Golgotha ˈgɔlgəθə

Goliath, –ases gəˈlaiəθ, -əsiz, *S* -ˈləiəθ

Goneril ˈgɔnəril

Gonzago gənˈzɑːgou, *It* gonˈdzaːgɔ

Gonzalo gənˈzɑːlou

>Stressed ‿ — ‿ T 5.1.68, unless that line has only four feet.

Goodman ˈgudmən

Goodrig ˈgudrig

Goodwin(s) ˈgudwin(z)

Gorboduc ˈgɔːrbədʌk

Gorgon ˈgɔːrgən

Goth gɔθ, *A +* gɔːθ, *S* gɔːt
  See *Sh.Pr.*, pp. 109, 234, 320.

Gower gauər, *S* gəur, gɔːr (?)

Grandpré grændˈprei, *S* grændˈpriː, *Fr* grãprę
  Spelled *Grand Pree* and *Grandpree* H5 F, *Gran Prie*
  H5 4.8.104 Q.

Gratiano ˌgreiʃiˈɑːnou, *A* ˌgræʃiˈɑːnou, ˌgrɑː-

Gratii ˈgreiʃiai, *S* ˈgreːʃiəi

Gray's Inn ˈgreiz ˈin

Graymalkin greiˈmælkin, -ˈmɔːlkin, *S* greːˈmɔː(l)kin,
  -ˈmælkin

Greece griːs

Green griːn

Greenwich ˈgrinidʒ, ˈgren-, *A* ˈgriːnwitʃ, ˈgrenitʃ

Gregory ˈgregəri, *S* ˈgreg(ə)ri

Gremio ˈgriːmiou, -mjou, ˈgremiou

Grey grei

Griffith ˈgrifiθ

Grindstone ˈgraindstoun, *S* ˈgrəinstoːn, ˈgrinstən

Grissel ˈgrisəl

Grumio ˈgruːmiou, -mjou

Guiana giˈɑːnə, *A*, *S* giˈæ(ː)nə

Guichard ˈgitʃərd, *Fr* giʃaːr

Guiderius gwiˈdiəriəs, -rjəs

Guienne giˈen

Guildenstern ˈgildənstəːrn, *S +* -staːrn

Guildford ˈgilfərd

56

Guildhall 'gild'hɔːl

Guiltian 'gilʃiən, 'giltiən

Guinover 'g(w)inəvər

> The same name as *Guinivere* ['g(w)iniviər].

Gurney 'gəːrni

Guy gai, *S* gəi

Guynes (*Guines*) giːn, *Fr* gin

Guysors (*Gisors*) dʒi'zɔːr(z), *Fr* ʒizɔːr

> The S spelling, unless due to false analogy, suggests [g-].

Hacket 'hækit

Hagar 'heigaːr, *S* 'heːgaːr

Hal hæl

Halfcan 'haːfkæn, *A, S* 'hæ(ː)fkæn

Half-moon 'haːf'muːn, *A, S* 'hæ(ː)f'muːn

Hames Castle (*Ham*, on the Somme) 'hæmz, 'heimz 'kaːsl, *S* 'heːmz 'kæːsl, *Fr* am

Hamlet 'hæmlit

Hampton 'hæmptən

Hannibal 'hænibəl

Harcourt 'haːrkərt, -kɔːrt

Harfleur 'haːrfləːr, *Fr* arflœːr

> The consistent F spelling *Harflew* may indicate that the final syllable was pronounced [fluː] in Shakespeare's time.

Ha'rford-west, see *Haverford-west*

Harpier 'haːrpiər, *S* 'haːrp(j)ər

> M 4.1.3, perhaps an error for *harpy*.

Harry 'hæri

Harvey 'haːrvi

Hastings 'heistiŋz, _S_ 'he:stinz

Hatfield 'hætfi:ld, _S_ -fi(:)ld

Haverford–west 'hævərfərd 'west, _S_ 'ha:rfərd 'west
>   Spelled _Harford-west_ R3 4.5.10 Q.

Hecate 'hekəti(:), _S_ 'hekit
>   Always disyllabic in S, except at 1H6 3.2.64.

Hector 'hektər

Hecuba 'hekjubə, _S_+ 'hekjube:

Helen 'helin

Helena 'helinə, _S_+ 'heline:

Helenus 'helinəs

Helias 'hi:liəs

Helicane 'helikein

Helicanus ˌheli'keinəs

Helicon 'helikən, -kɔn

Hellespont 'helispɔnt

Henry 'henri, _S_+ 'henəri
>   The trisyllabic variant occurs e.g. 1H6 2.5.82,
>   R3 2.3.16. _Fifth_, _Sixth_, and _Eighth_ were pronounced
>   [fift], [sikst], [e:t] respectively—cf. the F spellings
>   _Fift_, _Sixt_, _Eight_.

Henton 'hentən

Herbert 'hə:_r_bərt, _S_+ 'ha:rbərt

Hercules 'hə:_r_kjuli:z, _S_ 'hə:rkəle:z, 'ha:r-
>   See also _Ercles_ above, a variant used by Bottom
>   MND 1.2.31, 42.

Hereford 'herifərd, _S_+ 'hə:rfərd
>   Disyllabic at R2 1.1.3, 1.2.53, etc., and often spelled
>   _Herford_.

Herefordshire 'herifərdʃiər, -ʃər, _S_ 'hə:rfərdʃi:r

Hermes 'hə:_r_mi:z, _S_ 'hə:rme:z

Hermia 'hə:_r_miə, _S_ 'hə:rmie:, -jə

Hermione həːrˈmaiəni, *S* -ˈməi(ə)ni

    Trisyllabic WT 1.2.173, 5.3.28.

Herne həːrn

    The syllable *Her-* of the last four names may have been pronounced [haːr] by Shakespeare and his fellow actors.

Hero ˈhiərou, *S* ˈhiːroː

Herod ˈherəd

Hesperia hesˈpiəriə, *S* hiˈspiːrieː

    Spelled *Hisperia* AYL 2.2.10.

Hesperides hesˈperidiːz, *S* hesˈperideːz

Hesperus ˈhespərəs

Hiems ˈhaiəmz, *S* ˈhəiəmz

Hinckley ˈhiŋkli

Hipparchus hiˈpɑːrkəs

Hippocrates hiˈpɔkrətiːz, *S* -teːz

Hippolyta hiˈpɔlitə, *S* + hiˈpɔliteː

Hiren ˈhaiərən, *S* ˈhəirən

    See *Sh.Pr.*, pp. 114 f.

Hirtius ˈhəːrʃəs

Hob hɔb

Hobbididence ˌhɔbiˈdidəns

Hobgoblin ˈhɔbˌgɔblin, *S* hɔbˈgɔblin

Holborn ˈhoubərn

Holland ˈhɔlənd

Holmedon ˈhoumdən

    The place is now called *Humbleton Hill*; there is no clue to Shakespeare's pronunciation of *Holmedon* except that the name was disyllabic.

Holofernes ˌhɔloˈfəːrniːz, *S* + -ˈfaːrneːz

Hood hud

Hopdance ˈhɔpdɑːns, *A*, *S* -dæ(ː)ns

Hopkins ˈhɔpkinz

Horace ˈhɔrəs, -ris, *A* + ˈhɔːris

Horatio hoˈreiʃiou, -ʃ(j)ou, *S* hoˈreːʃo:

Horner ˈhɔːrnər, *S* + ˈhaːrnər

Hortensio hɔːrˈtensiou, -nʃiou, -nʃjou, *S* -nʃoː, -nʃioː, -nsioː

Hortensius hɔːrˈtensiəs, -nsjəs, -nʃjəs

Hostilius hɔsˈtiliəs

Hotspur ˈhɔtspəːr, *A* -ˌspəːr

Hour, Hower auər, *S* əur, oːr

Hubert ˈhjuːbə(ː)rt

Hugh hjuː

Hume hjuːṁ

Humphrey ˈhʌmfri

Hungary ˈhʌŋgəri

Hungerford ˈhʌŋgərfərd

Huntingdon ˈhʌntiŋdən, *S* ˈhʌntn̩dən

Hybla ˈhaiblə, *S* ˈhəiblə

Hydra ˈhaidrə, *S* ˈhəidrə

Hymen ˈhaimen, -mən, *S* ˈhəimən

Hymenaeus ˌhaiməˈniːəs, *S* ˌhəiməˈneːəs

Hyperion haiˈpiəriən, -per-, *S* həiˈpe(ː)riən, -jən

Hyrcan ˈhəːrkən

Hyrcania(n) həːrˈkeiniə(n), -njə(n), *S* (h)ərˈkeːnjə(n)

> The Q spelling *th'arganian* H 2.2.472 may indicate that the first syllable was pronounced [(h)ar-].

Iachimo aiˈækimou, *A* ˈjɑːkiˌmou, *S* ˈjækimoː, ˈdʒækimoː

> The name is always trisyllabic in S; see p. 22.

Iago (see p. 22) iˈɑːgou, *S* iˈɑːgoː

> Always trisyllabic, except perhaps at O 5.2.154.

Icarus ˈaikərəs, ˈikərəs, S ˈəi-, ˈi-

Iceland ˈaislənd, S ˈəislənd

Iden ˈaidn̩, S əidn̩

Ilion ˈailiən, -ljən, ˈiliən, S ˈəi-, ˈi-

Ilium ˈailiəm, -ljəm, ˈiliəm, S ˈəi-, ˈi-

Illyria iˈliriə, S iˈlirie:, -rjə

Imogen ˈimoʊdʒen, ˈimədʒən, S+ -dʒin

Inch(colm) ˈintʃ(kəm)

Ind(e) ind, aind, S ind, əind

    The second variant LLL 4.3.222, AYL 3.2.93.

India ˈindjə, -iə

Indies ˈindiz

Inverness ˌinvərˈnes

Io ˈaiou, S ˈəio:

Ionia(n) aiˈouniə, -njən, S əiˈo:nie:, -njən

Ipswich ˈipswitʃ

    The local pronunciation is [ˈipsidʒ], which S may
    have used.

Iras ˈaiərəs, S ˈəirəs

Ireland ˈaiərlənd, S ˈəi(ə)rlənd, ˈəirə-

    The name is trisyllabic H8 3.2.260; see p. 18.

Iris ˈaiəris, S ˈəiris

Isabel ˈizəbel, S+ ˈizbəl

    Spelled *Isbel(l)* AW 1.3.20, 25, 3.2.13, 15 and so
    pronounced MM 2.2.68, 2.4.144, 5.1.435.

Iscariot isˈkæriət

Isidore ˈizidɔ:r, ˈisi-

Isis ˈaisis, S ˈəisis

Isle of Man ˈail əv ˈmæn, S əil

Israel ˈizreiəl, S ˈizre:əl

Italy ˈitəli

Ithaca ˈiθəkə, S+ ˈiθəke:

Jack   dʒæk

Jacob   ˈdʒeikəb

James   dʒeimz

Jamy   ˈdʒeimi, *S* ˈdʒe(ː)mi

>   See *Sh.Pr.*, p. 186.

Jane   dʒein

Janus   ˈdʒeinəs

Japhet   ˈdʒeifet, *S* ˈdʒeːfet

Jaquenetta   ˌdʒæk(w)əˈnetə

Jaques   dʒeiks, dʒæks, *S* dʒeːks, ˈdʒeːkis, *Fr* ʒɑːk

>   *Jaques* is disyllabic [ˈdʒeik(w)is] AW 3.4.4, 3.5.98,
>   AYL 2.1.26, LLL 2.1.42 but can be either monosyl-
>   labic or disyllabic AW 3.5.37, AYL 2.1.41, 43, 54,
>   5.4.200, H5 3.5.43. There is no authority for the
>   current pronunciation [ˈdʒeikwi(ː)z] (see pp. 3, 18,
>   and *Sh.Pr.*, p. 330), nor, indeed, should any [w] be
>   sounded in *Jaquenetta* above.

Jason   ˈdʒeisn̩

Jenny   ˈdʒeni, *S* ˈdʒini

>   Spelled *Ginyes* (Jenny's) MWW 4.1.64.

Jephthah   ˈdʒefθə, *A* + ˈdʒepθə, *S* dʒeftə

>   Spelled *Jephta* H 2.2.422, 429.

Jeronimy   dʒəˈrɔnimi

Jerusalem   dʒəˈruːsələm

Jessica   ˈdʒesikə, *S* + ˈdʒesikeː

Jesu   ˈdʒiːzjuː, *A* + dʒiːsuː

Jesus   ˈdʒiːzəs

>   *Jesu(s)* may have been pronounced with [eː] in
>   Shakespeare's time; see p. 19

Jezebel   ˈdʒezəbl̩

Jill   dʒil

Joan   dʒoun

Job dʒoub, *S* dʒɔːb

John dʒɔn

Joseph 'dʒouzif

Joshua 'dʒɔʃwə, -ʃuə

Jourdain dʒuʳ'dein, dʒɜʳ'dein

    Spelled *Jordan(e)* 2H6 1.2.75 (verse, stressed ‿ ‑́),
    1.4.13 (prose).

Jove dʒouv

Judas 'dʒuːdəs

Jude dʒuːd

Jug dʒʌg

Jule dʒuːl

Julia 'dʒuːljə

Juliet 'dʒuːljət, -liət

    The trisyllabic variant is found only four times, at
    RJ 3.1.118, 5.3.73, 101, 302.

Julietta dʒuːl'jetə

Julio 'dʒuːljou

Julius 'dʒuːljəs

July dʒu(ː)'lai, *S* 'dʒuːləi

    Stressed ‑́ ‿ H8 1.1.154, WT 1.2.169.

June dʒuːn

Junius 'dʒuːnjəs

Juno 'dʒuːnou

Jupiter 'dʒuːpitər, *S* + 'dʒibitər

    For the colloquial variant with [i] for [uː] see *Sh.Pr.*,
    pp. 118, 211.

Justeius dʒʌs'tiːəs

Kate keit

Katharina ˌkæθə'riːnə, *S* ˌkætə'riːnə

Katherine ˈkæθ(ə)rin, *S* ˈkætərin, ˈkætrin

The disyllabic form occurs e.g. TS 2.1.62, 185.

Keech kiːtʃ

Keepdown ˈkiːpdaun, *S* -dəun

Kendal kendl̩

Kenilworth ˈkenilwə(ː)*r*θ, *S* ˈkilinwəːrθ

The name is spelled *Killingworth* 2H6 4.4.39, 44.

Kent kent

Ketl(e)y ˈketli

Kildare kilˈdɛə*r*, *S* -ˈdɛːr

Killingworth, see *Kenilworth*

Kimbolton kimˈboultən, ˈkimˌboultn̩, *S* ˈkiməltən

The F spelling *Kymmalton* H8 4.1.34 reveals the old local pronunciation [ˈkiməltən], now obsolete.

La Far ləˈfɑː*r*, *Fr* lafaːr

La Pucelle ləpju(ː)ˈsel, læ-, *Fr* lapysɛl

The F spellings *Puzel, Pussel* 1H6 seem to indicate a 16th-century pronunciation [ˈpʌzəl] or [ˈpʌsəl]; see also *Pucelle*, OED.

Laban ˈleibæn, -bən

Labeo ˈleibiou, -bjou, *S* ˈleːbjoː

Labienus ˌlæbiˈiːnəs

Lacedaemon ˌlæsiˈdiːmən, *S* ˌlæsiˈdeːmən

Lacies ˈleisiz

Lackbeard ˈlækbiə*r*d, *S* + ˈlækbɛːrd

Laertes leiˈəːrtiːz, *A* liˈəːrtiːz, *S* leːˈəːrteːz, liˈaːrteːz

The Q spelling is *Leartes*.

Lafeu, Lafew ləˈfjuː

Lammas ˈlæməs

Lamond ləˈmɔnd, *S* ləˈmuːnd

> The F spelling *Lamound* seems to indicate the use of [uː] for Fr [ɔ̃].

Lancaster ˈlæŋkəstər

Langley ˈlæŋli

Langton ˈlæŋtən

Lapland ˈlæplænd, *A* ˈlæpˌlænd

Lartius ˈlɑːrʃəs, *S* ˈlaːrʃəs

Launce lɑːns, lɔːns, *A* lɔ(ː)ns, *S* læːns, lɔːns

Launcelot ˈlɑːnslət, ˈlɔːns-, *A* ˈlɔ(ː)nsələt

> The F spelling *Lancelet* (beside *Launcelet*) may indicate a variant with [æː], which was probably also used in *Launce*.

Laura ˈlɔːrə

Laurence, Lawrence ˈlɔrəns, *A* + ˈlɔːrəns

Lavache (spelled *Lavatch* F) ləˈvætʃ

Lavinia ləˈviniə, -njə, *S* + -nie:

Lazarus ˈlæz(ə)rəs

Leah liə

Leander li(ː)ˈændər

Lear liər, *S* lɛːr

> The original form of the name, *Leir*, which S rendered *Lear*, suggests the pronunciation [lɛːr].

Le Beau ləˈbou, *S* ləˈboː

> The frequent F spelling *Le Beu* may imply a pronunciation [bjuː] on the analogy of *beauty*.

Le Bon (F *Le Boune*) ləˈbɔn, *S* ləˈbuːn (?), *Fr* ləbɔ̃

Leda ˈliːdə

Le Fer ləˈfɛər, *S*, *Fr* ləˈfɛːr

Le Grand ləˈgrænd, *Fr* ləˈgrɑ̃

Leicester ˈlestər

Leicestershire ˈlestərʃiər, -ʃər

Lena 'li:nə

Lennox 'lenəks

Leonardo li(:)ə'na:*r*dou, li(:)o-

Leonati li(:)ə'neitai, -na:ti:, *S* -'ne:təi

Leonato li(:)ə'na:tou

Leonatus li(:)ə'neitəs

Leonine 'li(:)ənain, 'li(:)o-, *A* 'li:ə͵nain, *S* -nəin

Leontes li(:)'ɔnti:z, *S* -te:z

Lepidus (see p. 20) 'lepidəs

Le Roy lə'rɔi, *Fr* lərwa

Lestrale le'stra:l, *Fr* lɛstral

    Perhaps stressed ⌐ — H5 3.5.45.

Lethe 'li:θi(:)

Lewis 'lu(:)is, 'lju(:)is, *S* lu:(i)s

    Regularly monosyllabic [lu:s] except at 3H6 3.3.169
    and perhaps 3H6 3.3.23, 4.1.29.

Libya 'libiə, -bjə

Lichas 'laikəs, *S* 'ləikəs

Licio 'liʃiou, 'lis-, *S* 'liʃio:, 'lis-

Ligarius li'gɛəriəs, -rjəs

Limander li'mændər

Limbo 'limbou

Limehouse 'laimhaus, 'liməs, *S* 'liməs

Lincoln 'liŋkṇ

Lincolnshire 'liŋkṇʃər, -ʃiər

Lingare 'liŋga:*r*(d)

    Holinshed has *Lingard*; cf. *Ermingare* above.

Lion 'laiən, *S* 'ləiən

Lionel 'laiənḷ, *S* 'ləi(ə)nḷ

Lipsbury 'lipsbəri

Lisbon 'lizbən

Livia 'liviə, -vjə, *S* 'livie:, -vjə

66

Lodovico ˌlɔdoˈviːkou, ˌloudəˈviːkou

Lodowick ˈlɔdowik, -də-, ˈlou-

Lombardy ˈlɔmbərdi, ˈlʌm-

Lombard Street, see *Lumbert Street*

London ˈlʌndən

Long Lane ˈlɔŋ ˈlein

Longaville (or *Longueville*) ˈlɔŋgəˈvil, *S* + -vəil

    It rhymes with *compile, mile* LLL 4.3.134, 5.2.54;
    see *Sh.Pr.*, p. 214.

Lorraine loˈrein, lɔ-, lə-

Lorenzo loˈrenzou, lɔ-, lə-

Louvre luːvr(ə), ˈluːvər, *A* + luːv, *S* ˈluːvər

Lovel(l) ˈlʌvəl

Lubbars Head ˈlʌbərz ˈhed

    Variant of *Leopard's Head*; see *Sh.Pr.*, pp. 41, 190.

Luccicos lu(ː)ˈtʃiːkəs, lju(ː)-

Luce ljuːs, luːs

Lucentio lu(ː)ˈsenʃiou, lju(ː)-, -ʃou, *S* -ʃio:

Lucetta lu(ː)ˈsetə, lju(ː)-

Luciana ˌluːsiˈɑːnə, ˌljuː-, *A* + ˌluːʃiˈænə

Lucianus ˌluːsiˈeinəs, ljuːʃi-, -ɑːnəs, *A* + -ˈænəs, *S* -ˈeːnəs

Lucifer ˈluːsifər, ˈljuː-

Lucilius luːˈsiliəs, ljuː-, -ljəs

Lucina luːˈsainə, ljuː-, *S* -ˈsəinə

Lucio ˈluːsiou, ˈljuː-, -sjou, -ʃ(j)ou

Lucius ˈluːʃəs, ˈljuː-, -siəs

Lucrece luːˈkriːs, ljuː-, *S* + ˈl(j)uːkriːs

    Stressed ⏑ — TA 4.1.64, TS 2.1.298, TN 2.5.116,
    and always in RL, except ll. 7, 512.

Lucretia luːˈkriːʃiə, ljuː-, -ʃə

Lucretius luːˈkriːʃəs, ljuː-

Lucullus lu:ˈkʌləs, lju:-

Lucy ˈlu:si, ˈlju:si

Lud lʌd

Ludlow ˈlʌdlou

Luke lu:k, lju:k

Lumbert Street ˈlʌmbərt ˈstri:t

Luna ˈlu:nə, ˈlju:nə

Lupercal ˈl(j)u:pərkæl, *A* + -ˌkæl, -kl̩

Lutheran ˈlu:θərən, ˈlju:-

Lycaonia ˌlaikeiˈouniə, *S* ˌləikeˈo:nie:

Lychorida laiˈkɔ(:)ridə, *S* ləiˈkɔ(:)ride:, -də

Lycurgus laiˈkə:*r*gəs, *S* ləi-

Lydia ˈlidiə, *S* + ˈlidie:

Lymoges (or *Limoges*) liˈmouʒ, *Fr* limo:ʒ

For the S form see p. 24.

Lynn lin

Lysander laiˈsændər, *S* ləiˈsændər

Lysimachus laiˈsiməkəs, *S* ləi-

Mab mæb

Macbeth mækˈbeθ, məkˈbeθ

Maccabaeus ˌmækəˈbi(:)əs, *S* -be(:)əs

Macdonwald məkˈdɔnəld, mæk-

Macduff mækˈdʌf, mək-

Macedon ˈmæsidən, -dɔn

Machiavel ˌmækiəˈvel, -kjə-, *S* ˈmækjəˌvel, -vil

The Q spelling *Matchavil* MWW 3.1.104 seems to imply a vulgar or colloquial pronunciation [ˈmætʃəvil].

Macmorris məkˈmɔris, mæk-

Madeira məˈdiərə

Maecenas mi(:)ˈsi:nəs, -næs, *S* me(:)ˈsi:nəs

Magnus ˈmægnəs

68

Mahomet mə'hɔmit, 'meiəmət, *S* 'meːəmət, -mit

Mahu 'mɑːhuː, *S* 'mɑːhuː, 'meː- (?)

Maidenhead 'meidn̩hed

Maine mein

Malchus 'mælkəs, *S* 'mɔːkəs

    The F spelling *Mauchus* points to the suggested S
    pronunciation.

Malcolm 'mælkəm

Mall mæl, mɔl

Malvolio mæl'vouljou

Mamilius mə'miliəs, -ljəs

Man, see *Isle of Man*

Manningtree 'mæniŋtriː, *S* 'mænintriː

Mantua 'mæntjuə, *A* 'mæntʃuə, -tuə, *S+* 'mæntjueː

    Sometimes disyllabic (e.g. RJ 3.3.169, 4.1.124), with
    -ua pronounced [ju], [wə], or possibly [ə]; see *Sh.Pr.*,
    p. 288.

Marcade 'mɑːrkə͵diː

    Clearly trisyllabic LLL 5.2.724, probably identical
    with Fr *Marcadé*.

Marcellus mɑːr'seləs

March mɑːrtʃ

Marcian 'mɑːrʃən

Marcius 'mɑːrʃəs, -ʃiəs

Marcus 'mɑːrkəs

Mardian 'mɑːrdiən, -djən

Margarelon mɑːr'gærələn

Margaret 'mɑːrgərit, 'mɑːrgrit

Margery 'mɑːrdʒəri, 'mɑːrdʒri

Maria mə'raiə, mə'ri(ː)ə, *S* mə'raiə, mə'riːə

Marian 'mɛəriən, 'mæriən, -jən, *S* 'mɛːr-

Mariana ͵mɛəri'ænə, -'ɑːnə, *S* ͵mɛːr-

Marina mə'ri:nə

Mark mɑ:rk

Marle mɑ:rl

Mars mɑ:rz

Marseilles mɑ:r'seilz, *S* ma:r'selə(s), *Fr* marsɛ:j
    The F spells it *Marcellus, Marcellæ*.

Marshalsea 'mɑ:rʃəlsi:, *S* 'ma:rʃəlse:

Martext 'mɑ:rtekst

Martino mɑ:r'ti:nou

Martius 'mɑ:rʃəs, -ʃiəs

Marullus mə'rʌləs

Mary 'mɛəri, *S* 'mɛ:ri

Masham 'mæsəm, 'mæʃəm

Matthew 'mæθju:

Maud mɔ:d

Maudlin 'mɔ:dlin

Mauretania ˌmɔ(:)rə'teinjə, -ri-, -niə, *S* -'te:njə, -nie:

May mei

Mede mi:d

Medea mi'diə

Media 'mi:diə, -djə

Mediterranean ˌmeditə'reinjən
    Spelled *mediteranium* LLL 5.1.61.

Meg meg

Meis(s)en 'maisən, *S* 'məisen

Meleager ˌmeli'eidʒər

Melford 'melfərd

Melun mə'lʌn, *S* mə'lu:n, *Fr* məlœ̃
    The S pronunciation is indicated by the F spellings
    Meloon(e), Melloone.

Memphis 'memfis

Menaphon 'menəfən

Menas ˈmiːnəs

Menecrates məˈnekrətiːz, *S* -teːz

Menelaus ˌmeniˈleiəs

Menenius məˈniːniəs, -njəs

Menon ˈmiːnɔn, ˈmenɔn

Menteith menˈtiːθ

Mephistopheles ˌmefiˈstɔfiliːz, -fəl-, *S* -leːz

> In MWW 1.1.132 Pistol says *Mephostophilus*
> [ˌmefəˈstɔfələs].

Mercade, see *Marcade*

Mercatio məˈrkeiʃou

Mercury ˈməːrkjuri, -kjəri, *S* ˈməːrkəri, ˈmaːr-

Mercutio məˈrkjuːʃjou, -ʃiou

> Four syllables RJ 3.1.142, 150, 187.

Merlin ˈməːrlin, *S* + ˈmaːrlin (?)

Merops ˈmerɔps

Merriman ˈmerimən

Mesopotamia ˌmesəpeˈteimjə

Messala meˈsaːlə, *A* meˈseilə, *S* meˈseːlə (?)

Messaline ˈmesəliːn

Messina (see p. 5, n. 2) meˈsiːnə, məˈsiːnə

Metellus miˈteləs

Mexico ˈmeksikou

Michael ˈmaikl̩, *S* ˈməikl̩

Michaelmas ˈmikl̩məs

Midas ˈmaidæs, -dəs, *S* ˈməidəs

Milan miˈlæn, ˈmilən

> Usually stressed ´ —, except possibly at T 2.1.132,
> where — ´. The F spells it *Millaine*.

Mile-end Green ˈmailend ˈgriːn, *S* ˈməil-

Milford Haven ˈmilfərd ˈheivn̩

Miller ˈmilər

71

Milo ˈmailou, S ˈmәilo:

Minerva miˈnә:rvә

Minola ˈminәlә

Minos ˈmainɔs, -nәs, S ˈmәinәs

Minotaur ˈmainәtɔ:r, S ˈmәi-

Miranda miˈrændә

Misanthropos miˈzænθropɔs, miˈsæ-

Misena miˈsi:nә

> Spelled *Mount-Mesena* AC 2.2.163, which most
> editors emend to *Misen(i)um*; North has *Misena*
> (today *Miseno*).

Mithridates ˌmiθriˈdeiti:z, S -ˈde:te:z

Mitigation ˌmitiˈgeiʃɳ

Mock-water ˈmɔkˌwɔ:tәr

> Since a pun is intended here (MWW 2.3.60–4), the
> first syllable should probably be [ˈmʌk-].

Modena moˈdeinә, -ˈdi:nә

Modo ˈmoudou

Moll mɔl, *A* + mɔ:l

Monarcho mɔˈnɑ:rkou, mo-, mә-

Monmouth ˈmʌnmәθ, ˈmɔn-

Montacute ˈmɔntәkju:t

Montague ˈmɔntәgju:, ˈmʌn-, *A* -ˌgju:

Montano mɔnˈtænou, -ˈtɑ:nou, S mɔnˈtæno:, -ˈtɑ:- (?)

Montferrat ˌmɔntfәˈræt, *Fr* mõfɛra

> The F spelling is *Mountferrat* MV 1.2.126, which
> may indicate S [ˈmu:nt-, ˈmәunt-].

Montgomery mәn(t)ˈgʌmәri, mɔn(t)ˈgomәri

Montjoy ˈmɔntdʒɔi, mɔntˈdʒɔi

> Both accentuations occur in H5, where the first
> syllable of the name is spelled *Mount-* and *Mont-*,
> the former probably indicating S [ˈmu:nt-, ˈmәunt-].

72

Moonshine 'mu:nʃain, *S* -ʃəin

Moorditch 'muərditʃ, *S* 'mu:rditʃ

Moorfields 'muərfi:ldz, *S* 'mu:rfi(:)ldz

Mopsa 'mɔpsə

Mordake 'mə:rdək

    This is Holinshed's spelling of *Murdoch*; S may therefore have pronounced it ['mə:rde:k, -dək].

More mɔ:*r*, *S* mo:r

Morgan 'mɔ:*r*gən

Morocco mə'rɔkou

Mortimer 'mɔ:rtimə*r*

Morton 'mɔ:rtṇ

Moses 'mouziz

    Spelled *Moyses* TGV 5.3.8.

Moth mɔθ, *A* mɔ:θ, *S* mo:t

    See *Sh.Pr.*, p. 320.

Mouldy 'mouldi

Mowbray 'moubrei, -bri, *S* 'mo:bre:, -bri

Mugs mʌgz

Muli 'mju:li

    F has *Muliteus* TA 4.2.152, which most editors emend to *Muli lives*; the F name may be pronounced [ˌmju(:)li'tiəs] or ['mju:litju:s].

Mulmutius mʌl'mju:ʃəs

Murray 'mʌri, *A* 'mə:ri

Muscovite 'mʌskəvait, *S* 'mʌskəvit

    Muscovits rhymes with *wits* LLL 5.2.264.

Muscovy 'mʌskəvi

Mustardseed 'mʌstərdsi:d

Mutius 'mju:ʃəs, -ʃiəs

    Disyllabic except at TA 1.1.389.

Myrmidon 'mə:*r*midən, -dɔn

Mytilene ˌmitiˈliːni, $S+$ ˈmetəlin, ˈmitəlin
> Trisyllabic P 4.4.51, 5.2.8, tetrasyllabic P 5.1.177; see further *Sh.Pr.*, p. 186, n. 5.

Naiad ˈnaiæd, ˈneiæd, S ˈneːæɑ
Nan næn
Naples ˈneipl̩z
Naps næps
Narbon ˈnɑːrbən
Narcissus nɑːrˈsisəs
Naso (see p. 20) ˈneizou, ˈnɑːsou, S ˈnˑːzoː
Nathaniel nəˈθænjəl
Navarre nəˈvɑːr, *Fr* navaːr
Nazarite ˈnæzərait, S ˈnæzərəit
Neapolitan niəˈpɒlitən, -tn̩
Nebuchadnezzar ˌnebjukədˈnezər, -bjə-, S ˌnebə-
Ned ned
Nedar (see p. 7) ˈniːdər
Nell nel
Nemean niˈmiːən, ˈniːmiən, S ˈnemjən, ˈniːmjən
> Disyllabic and stressed ⏑́ — in S; see *Sh.Pr.*, p. 338.

Nemesis ˈnemisis, -mə-
Neoptolemus ˌni(ː)əpˈtɒliməs, -ɒp-
Neptune ˈneptjuːn, -tʃuːn
Nereid(s) ˈniəri-id(z)
Nerissa niˈrisə, ne-, nə-
Nero ˈniərou, S ˈniːroː
Nervii nəːrviai, S ˈnəːrviˌəi
Nessus ˈnesəs
Nestor ˈnestɔːr, -tər

74

Netherlands 'neðərləndz

Nevil 'nevil, -vl̩

Newgate 'nju:git, -geit, S -git, -ge:t

Nicander nai'kændər, S nəi-

Nicanor nai'keinər, ni-, S nəi'ke:nər, ni-

Nicholas 'nikələs, A + 'nikləs
> Disyllabic ['nikləs] H8 1.1.221, 1.2.147, 2.1.96.

Nick nik

Nightwork 'naitwə:rk, S 'nəit-

Nile nail, S nəil

Nilus 'nailəs, S 'nəiləs

Ninny 'nini

Ninus 'nainəs, S 'ninəs
> With a pun on *ninny* MND 3.1.99–100.

Niobe 'naiobi, 'naiəbi, S 'nəi-

Noah nouə, nɔə, S no:ə

Nob nɔb

Norbery 'nɔːrbəri

Norfolk 'nɔːrfək

Normandy 'nɔːrməndi

Northampton nɔːr'θæmptən, A + nɔːrθ'hæmptən

Northamptonshire nɔːr'θæmptənʃiər, -ʃər

North-gate 'nɔːrθgeit

Northumberland nɔːr'θʌmbərlənd

Norway 'nɔːrwei, S 'nɔːrwe:

Norweyan nɔːr'weiən, S nɔːr'we:ən

Numa 'nju:mə, A + 'nu:mə

Nym nim

Oatcake 'out'keik

Oberon 'oubərən, -rɔn

Obidicut ou'bidikət

Octavia ɔk'teivjə, -viə, *S* ɔk'te:vjə, -vie:

Octavius ɔk'teivjəs, -viəs

Four syllables AC 3.7.73.

Oldcastle 'ould͵kɑ:sḷ, *A*, *S* -͵kæ(:)sḷ

Oliver 'ɔlivər

Olivia ou'liviə, -vjə, *S* o(:)'livjə

Olympus ou'limpəs

Ophelia ou'fi:ljə, -liə, *S* o(:)'fi:ljə, -lie:

Oracle 'ɔrəkḷ

Orlando ɔ:r'lændou

Orleans ɔ:r'liənz, 'ɔ:rliənz, *S* 'ɔ:rli(ə)nz, 'ɔ:rli͵ænz, *Fr* ɔrleã

The accentuation ‿ — ‿ occurs commonly at the end of a line.

Orodes ɔ'roudi:z, ou-, *S* ɔ'ro:de:z

Orpheus 'ɔ:rfju:s

Orsino ɔ:r'si:nou

Osric 'ɔzrik, 'ɔs-

Ossa 'ɔsə

Oswald 'ɔzwəld

Othello ou'θelou, ə'θ-, ɔ'θ-, *S* o(:)'telo:, o(:)'θelo:

Since the *th* of *Othello* ('little Otto') is a graphic variant of *t* (as in *Thomas*), *S* probably used the first of the two variants suggested here.

Ottomites 'ɔtəmaits, *S* -məits

Overdone 'ouvər'dʌn

Ovid 'ɔvid

Ovidius ou'vidiəs

Owen 'ouin, *S* o:in, -ən

Oxford 'ɔksfərd

Oxfordshire 'ɔksfərdʃər, -ʃiər

Pace peis

Pacorus 'pækərəs

Padua 'pædjuə, 'pɑːduə, *S* 'pædjuːe, -djuə, -dwə
    See note to *Mantua* above, and *Sh.Pr.*, p. 288.

Page peidʒ

Palamedes ˌpælə'miːdiːz, *S* -deːz

Palamon 'pæləmən, -mɔn

Palatine 'pælətain, *S* -təin

Palestine 'pælistain, *S* -stəin

Pallas 'pælæs, -ləs

Pandar 'pændər

Pandarus 'pændərəs

Pandulph 'pændʌlf

Pannonian pæ'nounjən

Pansa 'pænsə, -nzə

Pantheon (see p. 21) pæn'θi(ː)ən, 'pænθiən, *S* 'pænθjən

Panthino pæn'θiːnou

Paphlagonia ˌpæflə'gounjə, -niə, *S* -'goːnjə, -nieː

Paphos 'peifɔs

Paracelsus ˌpærə'selsəs

Parca 'pɑːrkə

Paris 'pæris

Paris Garden 'pæris 'gɑːrdṇ, *S* 'pæriʃ 'gɑːrdṇ
    Parish Garden H8 5.4.2 was the colloquial or vulgar
    pronunciation.

Parolles pə'rɔlis, -les

Parthia pɑːrθiə, -θjə, *S* 'pɑːrθieː, -θjə

Partlet 'pɑːrtlit

Patay pæ'tei, *S* pæ'teː, *Fr* patɛ

Patchbreech 'pætʃbriːtʃ, *S* -bri(ː)tʃ

Patience 'peiʃəns

Patrick 'pætrik

Patroclus pə'trɔkləs
Paul pɔ:l
Paulina pɔ:'lainə, *S* pɔ:'ləinə, -'li:nə (?)
Paunch pɔ:ntʃ
Peas(e)cod 'pi:zkɔd, *S* 'pe(:)skəd
Peaseblossom 'pi:z‚blɔsəm, *S* 'pe:z‚blɔsəm
Peck pek
Pedascule pi'dæskjuli:
Pedro 'peidrou, 'ped-, 'pi:d-
Peg-a-Ramsay 'pegə'ræmzi
Pegasus 'pegəsəs
Pelion 'pi:liən
Pella 'pelə
Peloponnesus ‚peləpə'ni:səs
Pembroke 'pembruk, *A* 'pembrouk, *S* 'pembruk
Pendragon pen'drægən
Penelope pi'neləpi, pə-
Penker 'peŋkər
Pentapolis pen'tæpəlis
Pentecost 'pentikɔst, *A* + 'penti‚kɔ:st
Penthesilea ‚penθesi'li(:)ə
Pepin 'pepin, *S* 'pipin, 'pepin, *Fr* pepɛ̃
    Spelled *Pippin(s)* H5 1.2.65 Q, LLL 4.1.122.
Percy 'pə:rsi, *S* + 'pa:rsi
Perdita 'pə:rditə, *S* 'pə:rdite:, 'pa:r-
Peregenia ‚peri'dʒi:njə
    This is the F form (MND 2.1.78); the Qq have
    Perigenia and North *Perigouna*, the latter of which
    is closer to the original Greek *Perigune*.
Pericles 'perikli:z, *S* 'perikle:z
Perigort 'perigɔ:rt, ‚peri'gɔ:rt, *Fr* perigɔ:r
Perkes pɑ:rks, *S* pa:rks

Undoubtedly an inverted spelling for *Parks*; for similar cases see *Sh.Pr.*, p. 250.

Perseus ˈpəːrsjuːs, -sjəs

Persia ˈpəːrʃə, *A* + ˈpəːrʒə, *S* ˈpəːrʃə, ˈpɑːrʃə

Peter ˈpiːtər

Peto ˈpiːtou

Petrarch ˈpiːtrɑːrk

Petruchio piˈtruːtʃiou, -tʃ(j)ou, *S* -tʃio:

The F spelling must be phonetic, with *ch* standing for [tʃ]. Hence the pronunciation [pəˈtruːkiou] should be avoided; see p. 22. In verse the name is trisyllabic except at TS 1.2.143, 2.1.71, 3.2.247, 5.2.111, and RJ 1.5.133, where it has four syllables.

Phaët(h)on ˈfeiəθɔn, -tən, *S* ˈfeːəθɔn, -tən

Pharamond ˈfærəmənd, -mɔnd

Pharaoh ˈfɛərou, *S* ˈfɛːro:

Pharsalia ˈfɑːrˈseiljə, -liə, *S* fɑːrˈseːljə

Pheasar ˈfiːzər, *S* + ˈfeːzər

Mrs. Quickly's corruption of *vizier*, for which see *Sh.Pr.*, p. 193.

Phebe ˈfiːbi

Phibbus, see *Phoebus*

Philadelphos ˌfiləˈdelfəs, -fos

Philario fiˈlɑːrjou, -riou, *S* fiˈlɑːrjo:

Philarmonus ˌfilɑːrˈmounəs

Philemon fiˈliːmɔn, -mən, fai-

Philip(pe) ˈfilip

Phillip, *Philippe*, and *Phelip* are early variants of *Philip*, a name borne by both men and women.

Philippi fiˈlipai, ˈfilipai, *S* fiˈlipəi

Always stressed ‿ ˊ ‿ in S (see p. 20).

Phillida ˈfilidə, *S* + ˈfilideː

Philo 'failou, *S* 'fəilo:

Philomel 'filomel, -lə-, *A* 'filə‚mel

Philomela ‚filo'mi:lə, -lə-

Philostrate 'filəstreit, *A* 'filə‚streit

Philoten 'failoten, -lə-, 'fil-, *S* 'fəi-, 'fil-

Philotus fi'loutəs, fai-

Phoebe 'fi:bi

Phoebus 'fi:bəs, *S* + 'fibəs

> *Phibbus* MND 1.2.37 is the form used by Bottom.

Phoenicia fi'niʃiə, fi:-, -ʃə

Phoenix 'fi:niks

Photinus 'fɔtinəs, 'fou-

Phrygia 'fridʒiə, *S* + 'fridʒie:

> *Phrygian* is always disyllabic ['fridʒən] in S.

Phrynia 'friniə, *S* + 'frinie:

Picardy 'pikərdi, -ka:*r*-

Pickbone 'pikboun

Pickt-hatch (or *Picked-hatch*) 'pikt‚hætʃ

Pie Corner 'pai 'kɔ:rnər, *S* 'pəi

Pierce piərs, pjə:rs, *S* pi:rs, pə:rs, pa:rs

Pigrogromitus ‚pigro'grɔmitəs, -grə-

Pilate 'pailət, *S* 'pəilət

Pilch piltʃ

Pillicock 'pilikɔk

Pimpernell 'pimpərnel

Pinch pintʃ

Pindarus 'pindərəs

Pippin, see *Pepin*

Pirithous pai'riθoəs, *S* pəi'riθoəs, 'pəiriθu:s

> Trisyllabic TNK 1.1.207 (probably), 1.3.55, 95
> and stressed ˈ — ˌ ; elsewhere four syllables and
> stressed — ˈ — ˌ .

Pisa ˈpiːzə

Pisanio piˈzɑːniou, -jou

 Trisyllabic in verse except at Cy 4.2.37, 317, where tetrasyllabic.

Pistol ˈpistl̩, *S* + pi(ː)sl̩

 For Mrs. Quickly's *Peesel* see *Sh.Pr.*, pp. 135, 215.

*P*ius ˈpaiəs, *S* ˈpəiəs

Placentio pləˈsenʃou

Plantagenet plænˈtædʒinit, -dʒə-

Plashy ˈplæʃi

 Today *Pleshey*, locally pronounced [ˈplʌʃi].

*P*lautus ˈplɔːtəs

Pluto ˈpluːtou

Plutus ˈpluːtəs

Po pou, *S* poː

Poi(c)tiers poiˈtiərz, *Fr* pwatjẹ

 The F spelling *Poictiers* for *Patay* 1H6 4.1.19 may imply that S used a pronunciation similar to the modern Fr form; see p. 24.

Poin(e)s poinz, *S* + points

 Spelled *Poines, Poynes, Pointz, Points* in F.

Poland ˈpoulənd

Pole, see *de la Pole*

Polemon poˈlemon, -ˈliː-

Polixenes pəˈliksəniːz, pɔ-, po-, *S* -neːz

Polonius pəˈlounjəs

Polydamas ˌpoliˈdæməs, poˈlidəməs

 The accentuation depends on whether we read "fierce" in "The fierce Polydamas" TC 5.5.6 as a disyllable or a monosyllable. The original Greek name was stressed _ _ ᷄ _.

Polydore ˈpolidɔːr

Polyxena pɔˈliksənə, pə-, *S* -əne:

Pomfret ˈpʌmfrit, ˈpɔm-

Pomgarnet pɔmˈgɑːrnit, pʌm-, ˈpɔm-, ˈpʌm-

Pompeius pɔmˈpiːəs

Pompey ˈpɔmpi

Pont pɔnt

Pontic ˈpɔntik

Ponton de Santrailles ˈpɔntən də sænˈtreil

> No certainty is possible; F spells the name *Ponton de Santrayle* 1H6 1.4.28, but the modern Fr form is *Poton de Xaintrailles*.

Popilius poˈpiliəs, -ljəs

Porpentine ˈpɔːrpentain, *S* -təin, -ti(ː)n (?)

Port le Blanc ˈpɔːrt lə ˈblæŋk, *Fr* pɔrləblɑ̃

Portia ˈpɔːrʃiə, -ʃə, *S* + ˈpɔːr-, ˈpɔːrʃie:

Portugal ˈpɔːrtjugəl, -tʃu-, *A* + ˈpoːrtʃəgl̩

Posthumus pɔstˈhjuːməs, poust-, ˈpɔstjuməs

> Usually stressed _ ´ _; for exceptions see p. 20.

Potpan ˈpɔtpæn

Pots pɔts

Poultney ˈpoultni

Poysam ˈpɔisəm, -zəm

Prague prɑːg, preig, *S* preːg

Prat præt

Prester John ˈprestər ˈdʒɔn

Priam ˈpraiəm, -æm, *S* ˈprəiəm

Priamus ˈpraiəməs, *S* ˈprəiəməs

Priapus praiˈeipəs, *S* prəiˈeːpəs

Priscian ˈpriʃiən

Procrus ˈproukrəs, ˈprɔkrəs

Proculeius ˌproukjuˈliːəs

Progne ˈprɔgni(ː)

82

Prometheus prə'mi:θju:s, pro-, -jəs

Propontic prou'pɔntik

Proserpina prou'sə:rpinə, *S* pro(:)'sə:rpine:

> The stress used at WT 4.4.116 is, however, not apparent; the form intended may well have been *Proserpine.*

Proserpine 'prɔsərpain, *S* -pəin

Prosper 'prɔspər

Prospero 'prɔspərou

Proteus 'proutju:s, -tiəs

> The name is trisyllabic TGV 1.2.14, 1.3.12, etc.

Ptolemy 'tɔləmi

Publicola pʌb'likələ

Publius 'pʌbliəs

Pucelle, see *la Pucelle*

Puck pʌk

Pudding 'pudiŋ, *S* 'pudn̩

Puff pʌf

Pygmalion pig'meiliən

Pyramus 'pirəməs

Pyrenean ˌpirə'ni:ən

Pyrrhus 'pirəs

Pythagoras pai'θægəræs, -gorəs, pi-, *S* pəi-, pi-

Queubus 'kju:bəs

Quickly 'kwikli, *S* + 'kwikləi

> A punning name in S; see *Sh.Pr.*, pp. 124, 220.

Quinapulus kwi'næpələs

Quince kwins

Quintus 'kwintəs

Quoint (see p. 19) kwɔint

Ragozine ˈrægəzi(ː)n

Rainold, Reynold ˈrenl̩d, *S* + ˈreːnl̩d

Ralph reif, rælf, *S* reːf

Ram ræm

Rambures ræmˈbjuərz

Ramston ˈræmstən

Rash ræʃ

Ratcliff ˈrætklif

Ravenspurgh ˈrævn̩spəːr(g), *S* ˈræ(v)nspəːr(g)
　　The name is disyllabic 3H6 4.7.8, R2 2.3.35, else-
　　where trisyllabic; see further *Sh.Pr.*, p. 326, and
　　PN YE, pp. 16 f., 19.

Reading ˈrediŋ, *S* ˈredinz
　　Readins MWW 4.5.80, as used by Evans, reflects
　　an earlier form of the name.

Rebeck ˈriːbek, *S* ˈrebik
　　Spelled *Rebicke* RJ 4.5.135.

Regan (see p. 3, n. 1) ˈriːgən

Reignier ˈreinjei, *S* ˈreːniːr, re(ː)ˈniːr, *Fr* rɛɲe
　　Stressed ⊿ — 1H6 5.3.131, etc., — ⊿ 1H6 1.2.61,
　　65, etc.

Reynaldo reiˈnældou, ri-

Reynold, see *Rainold*

Rheims riːmz, *S* reːmz, *Fr* rɛ̃ːs

Rhesus ˈriːsəs

Rhodes roudz, *S* roːdz

Rhodope roˈdoupi(ː), *S* ˈroːdopiː, ˈrɔdəpiː
　　Stressed ⊿ — ⊿ 1H6 1.6.22 (see p. 21).

Rialto riˈæltou

Rice ap Thomas ˈrais æp ˈtɔməs, *S* ˈrais

Richard ˈritʃərd

Richmond ˈritʃmənd

Rinaldo riˈnældou

Ringwood ˈriŋwud

Rivers ˈrivərz

Robert ˈrɔbərt

Robin (Goodfellow, Hood) ˈrɔbin (ˈgudˌfelou, ˈhud)

Rochester ˈrɔtʃistər, *A* + ˈrɔˌtʃestər

Rochford ˈrɔtʃfərd

Roderigo ˌrɔdəˈriːgou, *S* ˌrɔd(ə)ˈriːgoː

    Trisyllabic O 1.1.174, 184, etc.

Roger ˈrɔdʒər

Rogero rouˈdʒerou, *S* ro(ː)ˈdʒeroː

Romano (see p. 19) rouˈmaːnou, *S* ro(ː)ˈmaːnoː

Rome roum, *S* ruːm

Romeo ˈroumiou, *S* ˈroːmioː, -mjoː

Rosalind ˈrɔzəlind, *S* + -ləind

    From the multiple rhymes AYL 3.2.93–118 it ap-
    pears that in this particular case S wanted the
    syllable -*lind* to be pronounced [ləind], today [laind].

Rosalinda ˌrɔzəˈlində

Rosaline ˈrɔzəlain, *S* -ləin

Roscius ˈrɔʃiəs, -ʃəs

Rose rouz

Rosencrantz ˈrouzənkrænts, *S* ˈroːzinkrænts

    Spelled *Rosincrance* H 2.2.1, 33, etc.

Ross(e) rɔs, *A* + rɔːs

Rossill ˈrɔsil

Rossillion (*Roussillon*) rɔˈsiljən, ro-, ru-

Rotherham ˈrɔðərəm

Rouen ˈruːãːŋ, -aːŋ, -ɔ(ː)ŋ, *S* ˈroː(ə)n, *Fr* rwɑ

    Spelled *Roan* F and *Rone* Q H5 3.5.54; disyllabic
    only 1H6 1.1.65, monosyllabic H5 3.5.54, 64, 1H6
    3.2.16, etc., uncertain 1H6 3.2.1, etc.

Rougemont ˈruːʒmɔnt

    Spelled *Rugemount* R3 4.2.107 Q; for the relationship
    of *Rougemont* and *Richmond* see *Sh.Pr.*, p. 142.

Roussillon, see *Rossillion*

Roussi ˈrusiː, ruˈsiː

Rowland ˈrouljand

Rugby ˈrʌgbi

Russia ˈrʌʃə, *S* ˈrʌʃə, -ʃieː

    Trisyllabic MM 2.1.139.

Rutland ˈrʌtlənd

Saba ˈseibə, *S* ˈseːbə

Sackerson ˈsækərsn̩

Sagittary ˈsædʒiˌtɛəri

Saint Alban(s) sn̩tˈɔːlbən(z), *A* seint-

    The unstressed forms of *Saint* [sin(t), sn̩(t)], are
    rarely heard in A.

Saint Anne sn̩tˈæn

Saint Asaph sn̩tˈæsəf, -ˈæzəf, -ˈeizæf

Saint Bennet sn̩tˈbenit

Saint Clare sn̩tˈklɛər, *S* -ˈklɛːr

Saint Colme's Inch sn̩tˈkɔlmiz ˈintʃ

Saint Crispi(a)n sn̩tˈkrispi(ə)n

Saint Cupid sn̩tˈkjuːpid

Saint Davy sn̩tˈdeivi

Saint Dennis sn̩tˈdenis

Saint Edmundsbury sn̩tˈedməndzbəri

Saint Francis sn̩tˈfrɑːnsis, *A*, *S* ˈfræ(ː)nsis

Saint George sn̩tˈdʒɔːrdʒ, *S* + -ˈdʒaːrdʒ

Saint Gregory sn̩tˈgregəri, *S* -ˈgregri

Saint Jamy (see *Jamy*) sn̩tˈdʒeimi, *S* -ˈdʒe(ː)mi

86

Saint Jaques le Grand (see *Jaques*) sn̩*t*'dʒeik(i)s lə 'grænd, *S* -'dʒe:k(i)s, *Fr* sɛ̃ʒakləgrã

Saint Katharine sn̩*t*'kæθ(ə)rin, *S* -'kætrin

Saint Lawrence sn̩*t*'lɔ(:)rəns

Saint Luke sn̩*t*'l(j)u:k

Saint Magnus sn̩*t*'mægnəs

Saint Martin sn̩*t*'mɑːrtin

Saint Mary sn̩*t*'mɛəri, *S* -'mɛːri

Saint Michael sn̩*t*'maikl̩, *S* -'məikl̩

Saint Nicholas (see also *Nicholas*)   sn̩*t*'nikələs, *S* + -'nikləs

Saint Paul sn̩*t*'pɔ:l, *S* sn̩*t*'po:l

Saint·Peter sn̩*t*'pi:tər

Saint Philip sn̩*t*'filip

Saint Stephen sn̩*t*'sti:vn̩

Saint Valentine sn̩*t*'væləntain, -tin, *S* -təin

Saint Withold (see p. 8)   sn̩*t*'wiðəld

Sala (now *Ijsel*)   'seilə, *S* 'se:lə

Salanio, see *Solanio*

Salarino ˌsælə'ri:nou

Salerio sə'liəriou, -rjou, -'lerjou

Salic, Salique 'sælik, 'seilik

Salisbury 'sɔ:lzbəri, -bri, *A* + 'sɔ:lzˌberi

Samingo sə'miŋgou

Sam(p)son 'sæm*p*sn̩

Sandal Castle 'sændl̩ 'kɑ:sl̩, *A*, *S* 'kæ(:)sl̩

Sands sændz

The F spelling is *Sandys*, with the same pronunciation.

Santrailles, see *Ponton de Santrailles*

Saracen 'særəsn̩

Sardian 'sɑːrdiən

Sardinia sɑːrˈdinjə, -niə, *S* + saːrˈdinieː

Sardis ˈsɑːrdis

Sarum ˈsɛərəm, *S* ˈsɛːrəm

Satan ˈseitn̩, *S* ˈseːtn̩

Saturn ˈsætə(ː)rn

Saturnine ˈsætə(ː)rnain, *S* -nəin

Saturninus ˌsætərˈnainəs, *S* -ˈnəinəs

Saunder ˈsɔːndər, ˈsɑːn-, *A* + ˈsɔn-, ˈsæn-

Savoy səˈvoi

Saxon ˈsæksn̩

Saxony ˈsæksn̩i, -səni

Saxton ˈsækstn̩

Say sei, *S* seː

Scales skeilz

Scarlet ˈskɑːrlit

Scarus ˈskɛərəs

> The F spelling *Scarrus* may imply a pronunciation [skaːrəs] or [ˈskærəs].

Scone skuːn, *S* skoːn

> The rhyme *one*:*Scone* M 5.8.74–75 points to S [oː] (modern [ou]) in both words.

Scot skɔt

Scotland ˈskɔtlənd

Scroop skruːp

Scylla ˈsilə

Scythia ˈsiðiə, -θjə

Seacoal ˈsiːkoul, *S* ˈseːkoːl

Sebastian siˈbæstjən

Seely ˈsiːli

Seleucus səˈl(j)uːkəs

Semiramis səˈmirəmis, seˈm-, siˈm-

Sempronius semˈprouniəs, -njəs

Seneca ˈsenikə, *S* + ˈsenike:

Sennois ˈsenɔiz

Senoys ˈsenɔiz

Servilius sə(:)*r*ˈviliəs, -ljəs

Sestos ˈsestəs

Setebos ˈsetibɔs

Severn ˈsevərn

Sextus ˈsekstəs

Seymour ˈsi:mɔ:*r*

Seyton ˈsi:tn̩

    Seymour and *Seyton* may have had [e:] in S.

Shadow ˈʃædou

Shafalus ˈʃæfələs

Shakespeare ˈʃeikspiə*r*

    For the probable Elizabethan pronunciation see
    Sh.Pr., p. 177.

Shallow ˈʃælou

Shaw ʃɔ:

Sheffield ˈʃefi:ld

Shirley ˈʃə:*r*li

Shoetie ˈʃu:tai, *S* ˈʃu:təi

Shore ʃɔ:*r*, *S* ʃo:r

Shortcake ˈʃɔ:*r*tkeik, *S* ˈʃɔ:rtke:k, ˈʃɑ:rt-

Shrew ʃru:, *S* ʃro:

Shrewsbury ˈʃru:zbəri, -bri, ˈʃrouz-, *A* + ˈʃru:zˌberi, *S*
    ˈʃro:z-

Shylock ˈʃailɔk, *S* ˈʃəilɔk

Sibyl ˈsibil

Sibylla siˈbilə

Sicil ˈsisil

Sicilia siˈsiliə, -ljə

Sicilius siˈsiljəs, -liəs

89

Sicily ˈsisili

Sicinius siˈsiniəs, -njəs

Sicyon ˈsiʃiən, ˈsisiən

Sienna siˈenə

Sigeia siˈdʒi:ə, *L* siˈgeia

Silence ˈsailəns, *S* ˈsəiləns

Silius ˈsiliəs, -ljəs

Silver ˈsilvər

Silvia ˈsilviə, -vjə, *S* ˈsilvie:, -vjə

Silvius ˈsilviəs, -vjəs

Simois ˈsimouis, *A* + ˈsiməwis

Simon ˈsaimən, *S* ˈsəimən

Simonides saiˈmɔnədi:z, *S* səiˈmɔnide:z

Simpcox ˈsimpkɔks

Simple ˈsimpḷ

Sin(c)klo ˈsiŋklou

Sinel (see p. 7) ˈsainəl, *S* ˈsəinəl

Sinon ˈsainən, *S* ˈsəinən

Siward ˈsju(:)ərd, *A* + ˈsu:ərd

Skogan (F *Scoggan*) ˈskɔgən

Slender ˈslendər

Sly slai, *S* sləi

Smalus ˈsmeiləs, *S* ˈsme:ləs

Smile smail, *S* sməil

Smith smiθ

Smooth smu:ð

Smulkin ˈsmʌlkin

Snare snɛər, *S* snɛ:ɪ

Sneak sni:k

Snout snaut, *S* snəut

Snug snʌg

Socrates ˈsɔkrəti:z, *S* ˈsɔkrəte:z

Sol sɔl

Solanio sə'lɑːniou, -njou

Solinus sə'lainəs, *S* sə'ləinəs

Solomon 'sɔləmən

Solon 'soulɔn, -lən

Solyman 'sɔlimən

Somerset 'sʌmərsit, -set, *A* + 'sʌmərˌset

Somerville 'sʌmərvil, *A* 'sʌmərˌvil

Somme sɔm

Sophy 'soufi

Sossius 'sɔʃ(j)əs

Soto 'soutou

Soundpost 'saundpoust, *S* 'səundpoːst

Southam 'sauðəm, *S* 'səuðəm, 'sʌðəm

Southampton sau'θæmptn̩, sauθ'hæ-, *S* səu-

Southwark 'sʌðərk, 'sauθwərk, *S* 'sʌðərk

Southwell 'sauθwəl, 'sʌðəl, *S* 'sʌðəl

Sowter (see p. 7) 'suːtər, 'sautər, *S* 'səutər

Spain spein, *S* speːn

Sparta 'spɑːrtə

Speed spiːd

Spencer 'spensər

Sphinx sfiŋks

Spinii 'spainiai, 'spiniai, *S* 'spəiniəi, 'spi-

Spurio 'spjuːriou

Squash skwɔʃ, *S* skwɑʃ

Squele skwiːl

Stafford 'stæfərd

Staffordshire 'stæfərdʃiər, -ʃər

Staines steinz, *S* steːnz

Stamford 'stæmfərd

Stanley 'stænli

Star–chamber ˈstɑːrˈtʃeimbər

Starve–lackey ˈstɑːrvˌlæki

Starveling ˈstɑːrvliŋ, *S* ˈstɑːrvlin

Statilius stəˈtiljəs, stæˈ

Stephano (see p. 23) ˈstefənou

Stephen ˈstiːvn̩

Stockfish ˈstɔkfiʃ

Stokesly ˈstouksli

Stony–Stratford ˈstouni ˈstrætfərd

Strachy ˈstreitʃi, *S* ˈstreːtʃi

Strand strænd, *S*+ strɔnd

    Strond is used regularly in H8; see *Sh.Pr.*, p. 166

Strange of Blackmere ˈstreindʒ əv ˈblækmiər

Strato ˈstreitou, *S* ˈstreːto:

Styga ˈstaigə, *S* ˈstəigə

Stygian ˈstidʒiən, -dʒjən

Styx stiks

Suffolk ˈsʌfək

Sugarsop ˈʃugərsɔp

Surecard ˈʃuərˌkɑːrd, *S* ˈʃuːrˌkɑːrd

Surrey ˈsʌri, *A* ˈsəːri

Susan ˈsuːzn̩

Sutton Coldfield ˈsʌtn̩ ˈkouldfiːld, *S* ˈsʌtn̩ ˈko:fil

    For the F spelling *Sutton-cop-hill* 1H4 4.2.3 (*Sutton cophill* Q), in which *p-h* stands for *f*, see *Sh.Pr.*, pp. 298, 311.

Sweetheart ˈswiːthɑːrt

Sweno (see p. 7) ˈswiːnou, ˈswenou

Swinstead ˈswinsted

Swithold (see *Saint Withold* and p. 8) ˈswiðəld

Switzer ˈswitsər

Sycorax ˈsikəræks

Sylla ˈsilə

Syracusa ˌsirəˈkjuːzə

Syracuse ˈsaiərəkjuːz, ˈsir-, _S_ ˈsəirə-, ˈsir-

Syria ˈsiriə, _S_ + ˈsiriːe:

Talbot ˈtɔːlbət

Tale-porter ˈteilˌpɔːrtər

> For this name see _Sh.Pr._, p. 149.

Tamora ˈtæmərə, ˈtæmrə, _S_ + ˈtæməre:

> Apparently disyllabic TA 1.1.315, 319, 2.3.118, 293.

Tamworth ˈtæmwə(ː)rθ

Tapster ˈtæpstər

Tarentum təˈrentəm

Tarpeian tɑːrˈpi(ː)ən

Tarquin ˈtɑːrkwin

Tarsus ˈtɑːrsəs

Tartar ˈtɑːrtər

Taurus ˈtɔːrəs

Tearsheet ˈtɛərʃiːt, _S_ ˈtɛːrʃiːt

> For this name see _Sh.Pr._, p. 150.

Telamon ˈteləmən, -mɔn

Telamonius ˌteləˈmouniəs

Tellus ˈteləs

Temple ˈtempl̩

Tenantius təˈnænʃəs, te-

Tenedos ˈtenədəs, -dɔs

Tereus ˈtiːr(j)uːs, -riəs

Termagant ˈtəːrməgənt, _S_ ˈtɑːrməgənt

> Spelled _Tarmagant_ H 3.2.15 Q.

Tewksbury ˈtjuːksbəri, -bri, _A_ + ˈtuːksˌberi

Thaisa θeiˈisə, ˈθei-isə

> Stressed ◡́ — — P 5.1.212.

Thaliard 'θæljərd

Thames temz

Thasos 'θeisɔs, *S* 'θe:sɔs

Theban 'θi:bən

Thebes θi:bz

Thersites θə(:)r'saiti:z, *S* θə(:)r'səite:z

Theseus 'θi:s(j)u:s, -siəs

    Trisyllabic MND 2.1.76.

Thessalian θe'seiljən

Thessaly 'θesəli

Thetis 'θetis, 'θi:tis

Thisbe 'θizbi

Thoas 'θouəs

Thomas 'tɔməs

Thracian 'θreiʃ(j)ən, *S* 'θre:ʃən

Three-pile 'θri:pail, *S* -pəil

Thump θʌmp

Thurio 'θjuəriou, -rjou, *A* + 'θur-, *S* + 't(j)u:rio:, -jo:

Thyreus 'θaiəriəs, *S* 'θəiriəs

    Apparently disyllabic AC 3.12.31, 3.13.73.

Tib tib

Tiber 'taibər, *S* 'təibər

Tiberio tai'biəriou, *S* təi'bi:rio:

Tiger 'taigər, *S* 'təigər

Timandra ti'mændrə

Timon 'taimən, -mɔn, *S* 'təimən

Tisick 'tizik

Titan 'taitən, -tn̩, *S* 'təitən

Titania ti'teiniə, -njə, tai-, -'tɑ:n-, *S* təi'te:nie:, -njə

Titchfield 'titʃfi:ld

Titinius ti'tiniəs, -njəs, tai-

Titus 'taitəs, *S·* 'təitəs

Toby   'toubi

Toledo   tə'leidou, to-, *A* tə'li:dou, *S* tə'li:do:

Tom   tɔm

Tomyris   'tɔmiris

Topas   'toupəs, 'toupæz

Toryne (see p. 21)   'tɔrin

Touchstone   'tʌtʃstoun

Touraine   tu'rein, *S* 'tu:re:n
    Apparently stressed ⌣ — in S.

Tours   tuər, *S* tu:r(z), *Fr* tu:r

Tower   'tauər, *S* 'təur

Towton   'tautn̩, *S* 'təutn̩

Tranio   'trɑ:niou, -njou, 'trein-, *S* 'tre:nio:, -njo:, 'trɑ:n-

Transylvanian   ˌtrænsil'veinjən, ˌtrɑ:n-

Travers   'trævə(:)rz

Tray   trei, *S* tre:

Trebonius   tri'bouniəs, -njəs

Trent   trent

Tressel   'tresl̩

Trigon   'traigən, *S* 'trəigən

Trinculo   'triŋkjulou, -kjə-, *S* 'triŋkəlo:

Tripoli(s)   'tripəli(s)

Triton   'traitn̩, *S* 'trəitn̩

Troien   'trɔiən

Troilus   'trouiləs, 'trɔiləs, *S* 'trɔiləs, 'tro:iləs
    Always disyllabic in S, except at TC 5.2.161.

Trojan   'troudʒən, *S* 'tro:dʒən

Trot   trɔt

Troy   trɔi

Troyan   'trɔiən

Tubal   'tju:bəl, *A* + 'tu:bl̩

Tullus   'tʌləs

Tully 'tʌli

Tunis 'tjuːnis, *A* + 'tuːnis

Turk təːrk

Turkey 'təːrki

Turlygod 'təːrligɔd

Turnbull Street (i.e. *Turnmill St.*) 'təːrnbul 'striːt

Turph təːrf

Tuscan 'tʌskən

Tybalt 'tibəlt

Tyburn 'taibə(ː)rn, *S* 'təibə(ː)rn

Tymbria 'timbriə

Typhon 'taifən, *S* 'təifən

Tyre taiər, *S* təir

Tyrian 'tiriən, -rjən

Tyrrel 'tirəl

Tyrus 'taiərəs. *S* 'təirəs

Ulysses ju(ː)'lisiːz, *S* -'liseːz

Umfrevile 'ʌmfrəvil

Urchinfield 'əːrtʃinfiːld

Ursa Major 'əːrsə 'meidʒər

Ursula 'əːrsjulə, 'əːrsələ, *S* 'əːrsli, 'əːrsələ

 Spelled *Ursley* MA 3.1.4 Q, and always disyllabic
 in Shakespeare's verse.

Urswick 'əːrz(w)ik

Valdes (see p. 6) 'vældis, -əs

Valence 'væləns, *Fr* valãːs

Valencius və'lenʃiəs

 MM 4.5.8, which most editors emend to *Valentinus*.

Valentine ˈvæləntain, *S* -təin

Valentinus ˌvælənˈtainəs, *S* -ˈtəinəs

Valentio vəˈlenʃou, væ-

Valeria vəˈliəriə, -rjə, *S* vəˈliːrjə

Valerius vəˈliəriəs, -rjəs, *S* vəˈliːrjəs

Vapians ˈveipiənz

Varrius ˈværiəs, -rjəs

Varro ˈværou

Vaudemont ˈvoudmɔnt, *S* ˈvoːdmɔnt, *Fr* vodemɑ̃

Vaughan vɔːn, *S* ˈvɔːən

    Always disyllabic in S.

Vaumond ˈvɔːmənd

Vaux vɔːz, vɔ(ː)ks

Velutus vəˈl(j)uːtəs

Venetia veˈniːʃiə, *It* veˈneːtsia

    The F spellings *Vemchie, vencha* LLL 4.2.99 suggest
    some kind of anglicized pronunciation.

Venetian viˈniːʃən

Venice ˈvenis

Ventidius (see p. 22) venˈtidiəs, -ˈtidʒəs

    Spelled *Venti(d)gius* TmA 1.2.9, 3.3.3, 8.

Venus ˈviːnəs, *S* + ˈveːnəs

Ver vəːr

Verdun ˈvɛərdən, ˈvəːr-, -ˈdʌn, *Fr* vɛrdœ

    Stressed __ ´ in S.

Vere viər

Verges ˈvəːrdʒis, -əs, *S* ˈvaːrdʒis

    Usually given as [ˈvəːrdʒi(ː)z], which is an incorrect
    spelling pronunciation; the name is a colloquial **or**
    vulgar variant of *verjuice* and should therefore **end**
    in [dʒis] or [dʒəs]; see p. 3.

Vernon ˈvəːrnən

Veroles, Verollus vəˈrɔləs

The Q spelling *Verollus* P 4.2.115 reveals the contemporary pronunciation.

Verona vəˈrounə, *S* vəˈro:nə

Verones(s)a ˌvereˈnesə

Vice vais, *S* vəis

Vienna viˈenə

Vincentio vinˈsenʃiou, -ʃjou

Viola ˈvaiələ, ˈviələ, *S* ˈvəi(ə)lə

Disyllabic TN 5.1.251.

Violenta ˌvaiəˈlentə, *S* ˌvəiəˈlentə

Virgilia və:*r*ˈdʒiliə

Virginius və:*r*ˈdʒiniəs, -njəs

Virgo ˈvə:*r*gou

Visor ˈvaizə*r*, *S* ˈvəizər

Vitruvio viˈtru:viou

Volquessen vɔlˈk(w)esən

Volsce vɔls

Volscian ˈvɔlʃiən

Voltimand ˈvɔltimænd

Volumnia vəˈlʌmniə, *S* + -nie:

Volumnius vəˈlʌmniəs, -njəs

Vulcan ˈvʌlkən

Wakefield ˈweikfi:ld, *S* ˈwe:kfi(:)ld

Wales weilz, *S* we:lz

Wall wɔ:l

Wallon (now *Wallonie*) *S* wəˈlɔn (?), *Fr* valɔ̃

Walloon wɔˈlu:n, wə-

Walter ˈwɔ(:)ltə*r*, *S* ˈwɔ:(l)tər

Ware wɛə*r*, *S* wɛ:r

Warkworth ˈwɔ:*r*kwə*r*θ, *S* ˈwɑ:rkwərθ

Wart wɔːrt, *S* waːrt

Warwick ˈwɔrik, *S* ˈwarik

Warwickshire ˈwɔrikʃiər, -ʃər, *S* ˈwarikʃiːr, -ʃər

Washes ˈwɔʃiz, *S* ˈwaʃiz

Washford ˈwɔʃfərd, *S* ˈwaʃfərd

Waterford ˈwɔːtərfərd

Waterton ˈwɔːtərtn̩

Westminster ˈwestminstər

Westmoreland ˈwestmərlənd

White Hart ˈ(h)wait ˈhaːrt, *S* ˈhwəit ˈhaːrt

Whitefriars ˈ(h)wait ˌfraiərz, *S* ˈhwəit ˌfrəirz

Whitehall ˈ(h)waitˈhɔːl, *S* ˈhwəit-

Whitmore ˈ(h)witmɔːr, *S* -moːr

Whitsun ˈ(h)witsn̩, *S*+ ˈhwiːsn̩

    Spelled *Wheeson* 2H4 2.1.97 Q as used by Mrs.
    Quickly; see *Sh.Pr.*, p. 215.

Will wil

William(s) ˈwiljəm(z)

Willoughby ˈwiləbi

Wilnecot ˈwiŋkət

Wilson ˈwilsn̩

Wiltshire ˈwilt-ʃiər, -ʃər

Winchester ˈwintʃistər, *A*+ ˈwinˌtʃestər

Wincote, see *Wilnecote*

Windsor ˈwinzər

Wingfield ˈwiŋfiːld

Wingham ˈwiŋəm

Withold, see *St. Withold* and p. 8

Wittenberg ˈwitn̩bəːrg, ˈvit-

Wolsey ˈwulzi

Woncot (see p. 8) ˈ(w)uŋkət, ˈwɔŋkət

Woodstock ˈwudstɔk

Woodvil(l)e ˈwudvil

Worcester ˈwustər

> There is no need to read *Worcester* 1H4 3.1.5 as a
> trisyllable, for the line has ten syllables, although
> the two unstressed syllables at the caesura give the
> impression of a missing half-foot.

Wriothesley ˈrɔtsli

Wye wai, *S* wəi

Xant(h)ippe zænˈtipi

Yaughan jɔ:(ə)n

Yead Miller ˈjed ˈmilər

Yedward ˈjedwərd

Yorick ˈjɔrik

York jɔ:rk

Yorkshire ˈjɔ:rkʃiər, -ʃər

Zenelophon ziˈneləfən, zə-, -fɔn